Sharing Chagall

A MEMOIR

By

Vivian R. Jacobson

Chagallean wishes

Vivian R Jacobson

Vivian (Chaviva) Jacobson is that rare witness who still knew Marc Chagall personally and brought to us a living image of the man and his activities toward the end of his century (1887-1985). A lucid and emotional evocation of Chagall the humanist and visionary and Chagall the engaging late life artist of "the color of love."

- Benjamin Harshav (1928 - 2015)

The Jacob and Hilda Blaustein Professor of Hebrew and Comparative Literature, Yale University

Author of *Chagall and the Lost Jewish World* and *Chagall and His Times: A Documentary Narrative*

Published by Belleray Press
ravi@pinehurst.net
info@vivianjacobson.com
www.vivianjacobson.com

Library of Congress Control Number 2009905978
Library of Congress Call Number N6999.C46 J33 2009

ISBN Number 978-1-61539-727-3

Permission granted for reproduction of artwork, photos and use of Chagall quotations by ©2012 Artists Rights Society (ARS), New York/ ADAGP, Paris

Permission granted by Atlantic Permissions (The Atlantic Monthly) for use of quotation from July 1963 article by Carlton Lake

Text used with permission from Rizzoli International Publications, Inc. of Charles Sorlier's essay "In Memoriam" appearing in *Chagall: A Retrospective*, edited by Jacob Baal-Teshuva

Permission granted for use of portions of Dr. Joseph Aceves' review by ©2008 The Pilot, Southern Pines, North Carolina

Permission granted by Abbeville Press for reprinting of listing of Public Collections from Andrew Kagan's book, *Chagall*

Cover image: This Chagall original drawing with an inscription by the artist on the title page of the book *Chagall by Chagall* was given to Ralph Jacobson for his birthday in 1981.

Printed in the United States of America
Date of Printing – January 2010, First Printing
                    March 2010, Second Printing
                    December 2010, Third Printing
                    February 2012, Fourth Printing
                    January 2015, Fifth Printing
                    June 2016, Sixth Printing

Sharing Chagall

A MEMOIR

Marc Chagall, September 29, 1974

Photo courtesy of Morris (Moe) Spector

MARC CHAGALL

(1887 – 1985)

Marc Chagall was born into a Hasidic Jewish family on July 7, 1887, in Vitebsk, Belarus. The wonderful and vibrant memories of his early childhood were expressed in his artwork throughout his career. Oil paintings, ceramics, lithographs, posters, stained glass windows, tapestries, mosaics, book illustrations and works for the theater, ballet and the opera were the mediums in which he chose to express the human experience of life and love. In these different mediums he showed the magical realism that brought together biblical stories, people, angels, flowers, animals and musical instruments.

Major Chagall works live in cities and museums all over the world. Some of these are *The Jerusalem Windows* at the Hadassah Medical Center, the *Peace Window* at the United Nations, *The Four Seasons* mosaic and the *Job* tapestry in Chicago, murals for the Metropolitan Opera House in New York, and *The St. Stephan Windows*, Mainz, Germany. Throughout his career, Chagall, the greatest colorist in the 20th Century, had exhibitions in the major art institutions of the world. His many admirers found a spiritual connection to the artist. Like the subjects that he brought together in art, he brought people together to view his message of hope, peace, reconciliation and love.

The survivor of pogroms, anti-Semitism, the Russian Revolution, two World Wars and an escapee from the Nazis in 1941, Chagall still had hope for humanity and reconciliation. He never exhibited hate or anger for his oppressors. The way the world affected him personally deepened his determination to pour out his love for all people and to strive for understanding, hope, and peace, through his artistic talents. He brought this love to us in every artwork. Some people give so much to the world while they are living, that when they are no longer on this earth they continue to live in the hearts and minds of mankind. Such was the distinction and legacy of Marc Chagall.

INTRODUCTION

On July 7, 1887, in a small Russian village, a child was born who would become the famous and fascinating artist of the 20th century – Marc Chagall. And through a unique set of circumstances, it was my great good fortune to have his friendship for the last eleven years of his life, and to have the opportunity to work closely with him.

Let me take this opportunity to introduce you, the readers of this book, to the man who was a master in the world of art. Marc Chagall, however, was much more than a powerful force as a painter, sculptor and poet. He was a perceptive person with an intelligent, inquisitive mind, and a delightful sense of humor, and I want to share Chagall with you.

For the last thirty-eight years I have lectured on Marc Chagall in many parts of the United States as well as in Israel, France and Austria. Wherever I appear, people may not be familiar with my name, but they certainly do recognize the name of Chagall.

In the course of my lectures, by describing the social, political, religious, educational and family environment of Chagall, I have offered an insight of the artist, which in turn reveals the meaning and understanding of his paintings and other artwork. In addition, my personal stories of my friendship with Chagall have intrigued my audiences.

I first met Chagall when I was thirty-nine years old and he was eighty-seven. I am proud to have been on the periphery of his inner circle of friends, as the president of the American Association of the Chagall Biblical Message Museum and as chairperson of The Chagall Tapestry Committee for the Rehabilitation Institute of Chicago.

Now, in my eighties, I am one of the few living people able to relate the story about what it was like working with Chagall. I feel an immediate need to share my memories of the man and his ideas with an ever-widening audience. In addition, I have specially designed the outline, appendix and bibliography of this volume to give direction for the reader and student who may wish to pursue additional research on the artist. There have been many books written on Chagall the artist, but little has been written on Chagall, the person.

In the years that I have been lecturing on Chagall, I have sought to interpret and spread his message of hope, peace, reconciliation and love. Will this book inspire you to go out and work harder for a better world, as my friendship with Chagall has done for me? I would hope so. Nevertheless, as you turn the following pages, you will find a man who had an irresistible spirit, enjoyed life to the fullest, and is definitely a stimulating person with whom to spend a few hours – my friend, Marc Chagall.

Vivian Jacobson gives us a unique insight into Marc Chagall the person, as well as the artist. Chagall's passion for his work, his understanding of the healing power of art, and his enduring message for peace were major factors in his desire to contribute his talents to creating a better world. His art and his humanity touch people in all walks of life. Many thanks to Jacobson for sharing her experiences with one of the great artists of our time.

Carolyn Allen, North Carolina Humanities Council, former Resource Coordinator

Vivian Jacobson gives us a moving, charming, and loving memoir of Marc Chagall, the man and the artist. Her success in bringing the *Job* tapestry to Chicago is one of the many vignettes in the book that reveal her persistence and dedication to this artist and his message of love, hope, and beauty for mankind. You will share and understand her enthusiasm after reading this memoir.

Don A. Olson, Ph.D, Associate Professor, Department of Physical Medicine and Rehabilitation, Feinberg School of Medicine, Northwestern University

Finally a definitive look into Chagall the person, and a wonderful collection of nostalgic and touching stories that evoke the true spirit of the artist and the man. Vivian produced an appendix and bibliography, which will be an outstanding aid to any student, educator or researcher on Chagall.

Maurice Mahler,
Adjunct Professor for Olli-Ru Division,
Rutgers University and Art Historian

TABLE OF CONTENTS

Page

Chapter 1 – The First Meeting   1

Chapter 2 – A Bit of Background   7

Chapter 3 – Messages of Chagall   10

Chapter 4 – Musée National Message Biblique   16
        Marc Chagall

Chapter 5 – The Harpsichord   24

Chapter 6 – Reconciliation   31

Chapter 7 – The Women in Chagall's Life   40

Chapter 8 – The Undiscovered Chagall   49

Chapter 9 – Angel Stories   54

Chapter 10 – The Job Tapestry: The Beginning   62

Chapter 11 – The Job Tapestry: The Fulfillment   67

Chapter 12 – A Farewell   77

Chapter 13 – Moving Forward   82

Chapter 14 – A Gift to Chagall   91

Photographs   96

Acknowledgements   105

Appendix   107

Bibliography   151

Biography of Vivian R. Jacobson   159

DESCRIPTION OF CONTENTS

Introduction

Chapter 1 - First Meeting

This chapter describes my unexpected meeting with Marc Chagall in September 1974, and how I became the President of the American Friends of the Chagall Biblical Message Museum in Nice, France.

Chapter 2 - A Bit of Background

A look at my early years growing up in Chicago, how my background and experiences prepared me for the work with Chagall and laid the foundations for a remarkable and exciting friendship.

Chapter 3 - Messages of Marc Chagall

In addition to the underlying message that Chagall presented through his artwork of hope, peace, reconciliation and love, this chapter illustrates the important values that were continuously reflected in his way of life and in his art.

Chapter 4 – Musée National Message Biblique Marc Chagall

This chapter describes how and why the Museum was created, how it represents the epitome of Chagall's vision and dream for world peace. The chapter also deals with the part played by many significant people in Chagall's life to establish and maintain a museum and library devoted not only to his own artwork, but an expression of global art.

Chapter 5 -The Harpsichord

One of the principal treasures in the Museum is a replica of an 18th century French Blanchet harpsichord, on whose inside cover Chagall painted an image depicting the love story of the Biblical characters of Rebecca and Isaac. This chapter explains the complex steps necessary to complete the project that expressed Chagall's belief that an integration of music and art was necessary to bring peace in the world.

Chapter 6 - Reconciliation

Reconciliation was a major theme in Chagall's work. He designed stained glass windows for the apse of the St. Stephan Church, Mainz, Germany in 1973 was an indication of how strongly he believed in the theme of reconciliation between France and Germany and between Christians and Jews. The chapter describes how Chagall's work affected a few of the many who have been inspired by the windows, including my husband, who had fled Nazi Germany in 1939.

Chapter 7 - The Women in Chagall's Life and Other Reminiscences

To Chagall, the women in his life were a significant influence. In this chapter, I relate how important it was for him to touch and hold the hand of a woman, as well as sharing some personal reminiscences of my exceptional friendship with Chagall.

Chapter 8 - The Undiscovered Chagall

The world abounds with major artworks of Marc Chagall in notable galleries, museums and public places. However, in this chapter a glimpse is provided of the inconspicuous and more modest places in which a Chagall sketch, small painting, mosaic, stained glass window or other artwork may be found. Information about his poetry and writings is also included.

Chapter 9 - Angel Stories

From my very first meeting with Chagall to the time of publishing this book, my life has been profoundly affected by those whom I call Chagall Angels. In this chapter, I introduce the reader to a few of these 'angels' -- people who have provided support, help, and immediate assistance just at the right moment. They are truly like the angels that grace many of Chagall's paintings -- watching over, protecting and caring for me as I tell the Chagall story.

Chapter 10 - The Job Tapestry – The Beginning

The tapestry hanging in the lobby of the Rehabilitation Institute of Chicago is dedicated to the disabled people of the world. The drawing for the tapestry was completed when Chagall was 95 years old, and it became his last commissioned work. How the commission came about, as well as the events leading up to Chagall's agreement to do the work, is described in detail.

Chapter 11 - The Job Tapestry – The Fulfillment

This chapter is the account of the special committee that came together to raise the funds for the commission, a discussion of the methods used by the weaver to transform the Chagall drawings into the finished tapestry, and information regarding the unveiling of this unusual work are included.

Chapter 12 – A Farewell

When Chagall died at the age of 97, the world mourned. This chapter is devoted to my special recollections of that sad day in 1985 and to my visits to his grave site in St. Paul de Vence, France.

Chapter 13 – Moving Forward

The inspiration of Chagall led me to the lecture circuit beginning in 1978 and this chapter is devoted to some of my experiences as I have continued to bring the world of Chagall to life. It also describes a unique lecture presenting the commonalities of Chagall, the artist and Elvis Presley, the singer, that guided me to the commissioning of an initial piece of music combining the styles of the two 20th century icons.

Chapter 14 – A Gift to Chagall

For our golden wedding anniversary, my husband and I commissioned the same brilliant young composer to create a work based on the major themes found in Chagall paintings. The final chapter tells the story of this special gift.

For Ralph

Chapter 1
The First Meeting

It began with a series of telephone calls, and evolved into an unusual and rewarding friendship with an icon of the 20th century artistic world. The conversations were prompted by my lifelong interest in art, nurtured by trips as a young child to the Art Institute of Chicago, where I had first become fascinated with the works of Marc Chagall.

As time passed, Chagall's romantic paintings of flowers, floating lovers, angels and his autobiographical masterpieces of his early life in Russia, took on new meaning for me as I visited other museums. And, as a life member of the Chicago Chapter of Hadassah, I knew of Chagall's masterful interpretation of *The Twelve Tribes of Israel*, in the stained glass windows at the Hadassah Hospital Synagogue in Jerusalem.

In the early summer of 1974, Marc Chagall would visit Chicago for the dedication of his mosaic at the First National Bank of Chicago. The city already had in place sculptures by Picasso, Miro, Dufy and Calder, and now this very large mosaic created by Chagall and titled *The Four Seasons* was to be unveiled, a gift of Mr. and Mrs. William Wood-Prince in honor of his adoptive father, Frederick Wood-Prince.

If Chagall is going to be in Chicago, why couldn't the Chicago Chapter of Hadassah have a fund raising event with Chagall as the honored guest, I wondered. The problem was that although I had met Mrs. Wood-Prince briefly some years before, I didn't have her unlisted telephone number.

Our brief encounter came when I was working as a volunteer coordinator on an election campaign for Senator Charles Percy. I clearly recalled the gracious, sincere and elegant woman. What a sight it was to see her silver chauffeur-driven Rolls Royce parked under the Chicago "El" tracks while she energetically stuffed and addressed envelopes.

Through the good graces of Senator Percy, I got the necessary number and called Eleanor Wood-Prince. After inquiring if she thought my idea had any merit, she suggested that I write a note in French extending the invitation which she would give it to Chagall personally.

I neither told my husband what I had done, nor the president of the chapter, Mrs. Dellsy. I kept it to myself, because I knew that there was little chance of Chagall and his wife, Vava, accepting the invitation. The media had printed the itinerary for Chagall, and it appeared that there would not be a moment available for my dream to become a reality.

Several weeks later, Mrs. Wood-Prince called to let me know that the Chagalls had accepted the invitation. She explained there were special conditions that would have to be strictly observed. First, the reception was to take place in our home the Sunday after the dedication of the mosaic. Second, absolutely no newspaper, television or radio coverage of the event was to be allowed. Third, that only twelve people (including the Chagalls and the Wood-Princes) could attend the reception. The fourth stipulation concerned what would be served at the reception. Since Chagall liked several different kinds of sweets, especially chocolate, the selection should include a choice of chocolate pastries and candies, the coffee should be light, and the tea very strong.

Having inhaled these instructions with absolute delight, I exhaled as I wondered how I was going to invite only eight Hadassah women to my home, when there were thousands in Chicago and the suburbs. Putting that thought aside for the moment, I excitedly called my husband, Ralph, an attorney for Sears, Roebuck and Co., to relay the incredible news and to tell him about the honored guests we would be greeting on a September Sunday.

His reaction? As always he had an utterly practical approach. "Start cleaning the house immediately, inside and out!"

Mrs. Dellsy's response was one of stunned silence. After I explained the conditions to her, she came up with an excellent solution. Her strategy was to invite the two families, the Goldenbergs and the Rosensteins, who had each donated substantial sums towards the stained glass windows in Jerusalem. Moreover, she wanted to pay tribute to Marc Chagall by installing him as a Hadassah Associate, the men's auxiliary. Sunday, September 29, 1974, was a perfect early fall day. The neighborhood in which we lived was absolutely tranquil as if the Chicago police had known about the momentous occasion and had placed a cordon around the block. Time seemed to stand still after we completed all the preparations and awaited the 4 p.m. arrival of our guests of honor, Marc and Vava Chagall and the Wood-Princes.

In order to keep the gathering unpublicized, I had asked the other guests to come at 3 p.m. I told them I would call them just before they left to come

2

to our house and at that time I would announce who the guests of honor would be.

At about 3:45 I left the guests and my family, as I wanted to be outside waiting on the corner by myself. As I stood there, I thought why is Marc Chagall making an effort to come to a small Hadassah reception, when he must have had a dozen invitations for this afternoon after the public dedication of the mosaic?

It was years later that I found my answer. Chagall had always admired the volunteer work of the Hadassah women, and fondly remembered the woman, Dr. Miriam Freund, the national president of the organization who had commissioned the stained glass windows at the Hadassah Hospital Synagogue in Jerusalem. While Chagall had previously done windows for several large churches, finally with the Jerusalem windows, he received recognition by the Jewish people with a major commission for a synagogue.

But that revelation was still far in the future. For that Sunday in 1974 I had ransacked my closet, changing my mind several times about what to wear before choosing a simple black velvet dress with a white collar. As a gesture of welcome I had placed my mother's treasured red porcelain vase inlaid with sterling silver containing beautiful gladioli blooms in a prominent place in the living room.

The tea table was set with a silver service purchased in Israel, and laden with a mouth-watering assortment of sweets. I had never excelled at preparing cakes, pastries, and confections, so when I invited the guests, I called on the other women of Hadassah, who are known for their wonderful baking skills, to provide a delicious variety of treats.

My first impression of Chagall was how young he looked for his age. He was wearing a blue coat, scarf, and small hat with a narrow brim. No sign of a cane, glasses, or a hearing aid. Walking up the steps with him, I couldn't believe he was a man in his late eighties. And Vava made just as handsome an impression as her husband, Marc. Stunning in her appearance, with her beautiful silky gray hair fashioned into a chignon at the back of her neck, she was a match for Chagall.

Marc and Vava Chagall had been entertained royally during their stay in Chicago, and had spent some time with the Wood-Princes at their quiet summer retreat in Gurnee, Illinois. The honor of hosting Marc and Vava Chagall was enhanced by the privilege of welcoming the Wood-Princes, the movers and shakers of Chicago's art world, to our home. Mr. Wood-Prince cut a dashing country squire-like figure in a sport jacket and open-necked shirt with a colorful ascot, and Mrs. Wood-Prince was tastefully dressed in an elegant blue silk suit.

After I formally welcomed Chagall with a small speech in French, Mrs. Dellsy placed a Hadassah Associate pin on Chagall's lapel and presented him with a plaque signifying his membership. He was delighted with these symbols of friendship.

Chagall, in his tweed sport coat, knitted gray vest and navy blue shirt, greeted each guest with his marvelous blue eyes, and graciously signed books about his artwork that the guests had brought. An amusing incident that took place after the conversation began to flow freely concerned a painting that hung in our living room.

I had picked up the painting by an unknown French artist on a trip to Paris some years before, as a gift for my husband. Ralph, however, didn't like the work, so he took this opportunity to ask for Chagall's opinion of the painting. Standing before the painting, Chagall studied it, and then never said a word. He just screwed up his eyes, shook his head, and waved a pointed finger in a downward motion. I learned right then that Chagall could express his emotions without speaking a syllable.

When Chagall was leaving the house at the end of the party, he stopped on the sidewalk, turned to Ralph and pronounced in German, "Ah, frische luft!" (Ah, fresh air!), capturing the lovely fall weather in just two words. Although Chagall was conversant in several languages, as both Ralph and I realized that day, Chagall believed in using language carefully, often depending on body language and a scarcity of phrases to convey his thoughts.

At first I had continued to speak in French to Chagall, but then I flowed right into Yiddish. It was so natural for both of us, and I believe that this was the moment that our friendship began. There is a saying that the Yiddish language can do wonders in bringing people together. It does.

The visit with our special guests was truly wonderful and memorable, especially for our two sons, Daniel and Ernest, who were fourteen and sixteen years old. They were in awe, but Chagall put them at ease with quiet conversation and ever present smiles. Our Hadassah guests were thrilled to meet the man whose great work they had so generously supported. Ralph and I were pleased beyond our wildest dreams, and I hoped that more exciting meetings with Chagall might follow.

Little did I realize on that special day that for the next eleven years I would become intricately involved in the life and the work of Chagall. Mrs. Wood-Prince approached me several months after our intimate reception and laid out her plans for a new association she was establishing in the United States to represent The Chagall Biblical Message Museum in Nice, France "I want you to become its secretary," Eleanor Wood-Prince told me. It didn't take me more than a split-second to accept the position, and then six months later I became the president of the organization upon her request.

The purpose of The American Friends of the Chagall Biblical Message Museum was primarily one of fund-raising through a widening appreciation of the works of Chagall. His artistic talents encompassed so much more than his brilliant paintings. His stained glass windows and mosaics were complemented by his remarkable costume and set designs for theater and ballet companies. His gifts extended into every creative medium - lithographs, book illustrations, tapestries and ceramics.

The goal was to increase membership in the Museum through the sale of signed Chagall posters, the planning and implementation of concerts, exhibitions, use of its extensive library, with every aspect and endeavor carried out according to the wishes of Chagall. The walls of the Museum are graced with Chagall's seventeen major works based on the Old Testament chapters of *Genesis, Exodus* and the *Song of Songs*.

Reflecting his conviction that the Bible was the most important book ever written, Chagall returned to it time and time again for inspiration. Chagall used his art as a medium to bring a message of hope, peace, reconciliation and love to the world.

During the years of my presidency of the American Friends of the Museum, I traveled several times a year to visit Chagall, and brought groups of people from the United States to the Museum and to Switzerland, Germany and Israel to view the whole range of Chagall's artistic genius.

I always brought him the wonderful Frango Chocolate Mints from Marshall Fields that Chagall doted on, and he always spoke with enthusiasm about Chicago. In fact, on one occasion several years after the trip which began our friendship, he proclaimed, "J'aime Chicago, J'aime Chicago! Je voudrais la voir encore une fois." (I love Chicago. I love Chicago! I wish to visit again).

5

His remarks came at a small gathering of friends having afternoon tea at his home, and I was privileged to be included that day. I was sitting on a sofa bench between Chagall and Vava, and Chagall was holding my hand. Upon hearing his passionate feelings for my city, I turned to Vava, and commented, in English, "Ralph cannot wait for you to come back to Chicago, because our house hasn't been as clean as the day you came to visit us."

Everyone in the room laughed. Chagall, however, was disturbed because he didn't understand my English quip. Vava then leaned over and translated it into Russian. Without missing a beat, Chagall told me, "Je vous donne six mois." (I will give you six months). Such was the quickness of his wit and his keen sense of humor.

It was an exciting time to be in the presence of such a great personality and to have him hold my hand and thank me for all the volunteer work that I had done for him and the museum.

As strange as it may sound, in retrospect I think that nothing prepared me for this prestigious leadership role more than my years as a swimming instructor, an instructor/trainer, a director of waterfronts for Jewish camps in the United States and volunteer swimming teacher in the kibbutzim of Israel.

Chapter 2
A Bit of Background

Growing up in a Jewish home with the solemn observances of the Friday night Sabbath and the traditional Jewish holidays, coupled with my years as a Hebrew student at the Anshe Ernet Synagogue and the College of Jewish Studies in Chicago, I had the foundation for my becoming the president of the American Friends of the Chagall Biblical Message Museum.

I became fluent in Yiddish at an early age, thanks to my grandmother, Peshe Epstein, who lived in my parent's home. She was a formidable woman and a great influence on my life and that of my sister, Charlotte, spoiling both of us to no end. She did not speak English. From her love and devotion communicated so profoundly in Yiddish in my childhood that I grew up becoming proficient in her language, and loving to listen to her rich speech and unique expressions.

My father had come to the United States from Kishniev, Russia in 1920, while my mother, who was born in Lodz, Poland, had been in the United States since 1906. We occupied an apartment that is known as a "railroad flat" with all the rooms leading off a long hallway. In my childish enthusiasm, I took delight racing up and down that hallway which earned me the family nickname "Vilde Chayah," translated freely into "Tornado".

About the time I turned nine, my parents decided to curb that unruly behavior by entering me in a Saturday children's clay modeling class at the Art Institute of Chicago. One of the advantages of the plan was my parents would have several hours of a quiet and peaceful Sabbath. Neatly dressed, I took the bus by myself to the historic building at Michigan Avenue and Adams Street, and joined several dozen youthful beginning sculptors.

Patience was never my long suit, and I quickly became bored with the lengthy explanations about technique to which the class was subjected. Raising my hand, in a loud whisper I indicated I needed to go to the wash room, and escaped the confinement of the classroom.

I never went back. I found the stairs to the upper floors and the world of art opened before me on that day. I wandered the halls of the museum.

In my wildest childhood imaginations, I hadn't conceived of such beauty.

There Chagall's *White Crucifixion* first spoke to me. Although I didn't realize it at that time, later on I would grasp the full impact of the image that had stirred my mind and heart. I asked myself why would a Jew paint the Christ configuration, not knowing that I had virtually met the artist through the significance of his ideas.

From the time I was seven until I became thirteen, after school I would take the streetcar to the Anshe Emet Synagogue for two hours of study on Monday through Thursday and three hours on Sunday morning of Hebraic, Biblical and Judaic studies. At this great institution I was immersed in learning to read and write Hebrew. During the ensuing years at high school, I continued my Hebrew studies at the College of Jewish Studies.

Two of my uncles, Albert K. Epstein and Benjamin R. Harris, who were very prominent in the Chicago Jewish community, had determined that I should attend a Hebrew-speaking camp in the northern woods of Wisconsin. As a result my pre-teen and adolescent summers were spent at Camp Ramah. There I learned to speak Hebrew fluently, supplemented by an intensive study of the Bible, Jewish history, and literature.

The educational experiences at Anshe Emet synagogue, the College of Jewish Studies and Camp Ramah served me well as I embarked on my journey of friendship with Marc Chagall.

I didn't have any formalized background or talent in art. I was not a curator of a museum, an art historian, or an author of books on art. All I could bring to the relationship were my cultural and religious teachings, as well as my occupational resources as a swimming instructor, aquatic lecturer and consultant, who happened to love the works of Chagall.

I really felt that Chagall admired me as an "outsider" and believed my love of Israel and the Jewish people were sufficient credentials for being the American president of the association of his cherished museum.

As soon as I became president, I enrolled at Northeastern Illinois University to do post-graduate work in the French language, literature and culture. I wanted to be able to freely converse with Chagall, together with the director of the museum, Pierre Provoyeur and his staff, and also to be able to carry on correspondence in French.

When I went to visit Chagall, I would greet him as "Maître", (or Master) and in the beginning he referred to me as Madame Jacobson. However, within a very short time, he called me by my Hebrew name, "Chaviva."

Initially, I spoke in French, but on my second visit, he encouraged me to speak in Yiddish as I had done at our first meeting. He said to me, "Far vas redstu tsu mir in Frantzayzish, ven vir kenen redn oyf Yiddish." "Why are you speaking to me in French, when we can speak in Yiddish?" And so it became our language.

One day I was with a group of people in Chagall's residence, and started to speak Yiddish to him. Why not? That is what he had requested. He gently took my arm and led me to a corner of the room and said, "Far vos redstu mir oyf Yiddish, tsu fil mentshen dorten, redn tsu mir oyf Frantza-yzish." I don't think any translation is needed and from that time on, we spoke Yiddish only when we were alone. He definitely wanted to speak French when other people were present.

Vava Chagall always greeted me warmly at the door of their home in St. Paul de Vence. I would sit and wait for him in his splendid living room in anticipation to tell him of another painting that I so admired.

Chagall had few words to say about his own work. He wanted the view-er to make up his or her own mind about each piece. In other words, he expected the viewer to have an actual conversation with the artist through his painting, defining what his/her emotional response was to the work.

Sometimes I would mention to Chagall that I was struck by a specific color or interpretation in one of his works. He would not respond, but I knew that he was pleased because he would have a marvelous twinkle in his eye and a broad smile on his face.

Marc Chagall, for the most part, let his emotions and actions speak for him. Our conversations never started with "Hello, how are you?" or a discussion of the weather. They contained none of the usual platitudes. Very often, he would greet me with a smile and pat my cheek with his four fingers. Then he would get right to the point of what he wanted to say.

Of course, conversing in Yiddish helped to rule out any misunderstand-ings because it is a language that comes from the heart. I can recall details of Chagall's actions and emotions much more clearly than I can relay actual conversations. An unspoken bond existed between us. In these very private moments that Chagall would hold my hand, is a memory that I will always cherish.

Chapter 3
The Messages of Chagall

Chagall's legacy isn't just bound by the magnificent works of art he created over his lifetime. As I explored the true nature of the man behind the great artist, I realized that his life was full of messages, and we can better our own lives by becoming receptive to what his life can teach us.

Chagall believed that there would be world peace through the integration of art and music. I have often wondered how he would have handled the current situation in the Middle East. In my imagination he would transport the New York Philharmonic or the Chicago Symphony Orchestra to Kabul, Baghdad or the Gaza Strip, and would have them play a Mozart or Beethoven symphony. He would have people marching around holding up not only his paintings but other artistic masterpieces. That would stop the fighting!

Getting back to reality, though, I know that Chagall, despite the very dark periods in his own life, had an unwavering trust in hope, faith and courage. He believed in miracles and the infinite wisdom of a Creator.

I have been asked many times if Chagall, as a Jew, was a religious person. He did not practice his religion praying three times a day, observing dietary restrictions, attending services or observing the holy days. He was a very spiritual person. It was through his immense artistic output that he constantly brought a message of joy and the hope for a better tomorrow and that productivity became his religion.

Chagall, in describing his philosophy said, "In our life, there is a single color, as on an artist's palette, which provides the meaning of life and art. It is the color of love."

Another one of his credos was never forgetting your past, letting people know where you came from and sharing those precious moments with others. Chagall was proud of his heritage. His powerful feeling for his native Vitebsk, a city in Belarus that was present in so many of his works, was his method of sharing his past with the viewer.

His mother and father, whom he considered holy people, his brother, six sisters, his relatives, the rabbis, the synagogue, the scenes of his village became his subjects as a beautifully conceived pictorial history of the

Hasidic Jewish life in the latter part of the 19th century and the early years of the 20th century.

No matter how famous he became, no matter the hundreds of thousands of people who came to his exhibitions and the major awards given to him by Italy, France, Israel, and the United States, Chagall never forgot the life and the spirit of the people of Vitebsk. Chagall commented, "In my pictures there is not one centimeter free from nostalgia of my native land."

Chagall lived when the Age of Enlightenment had started in France and swept across Europe to Russia. This provided him with a vision to step outside his tightly constricted Hasidic background. He sought to learn about the world beyond his limited experience, and at first was drawn by the colors, the artwork, and the sacred ornaments he discovered in the Russian Orthodox Church.

Chagall began to follow his artistic visions and created works that were like poetry in radiant colors and shapes. He painted angels, lovers, fiddlers, circus performers and denizens of the animal kingdom, all representing the beauty of creation. No matter what was happening in the outside world, he didn't let it affect his artistic efforts.

Above all, Chagall didn't paint with just a paintbrush, he painted with his heart. He was passionate about every aspect of life, and he never ceased bringing joy to the world.

An incident that brought another of Chagall's messages home to me took place at a special exhibition of his work, entitled "Works on Paper" held at the Centre Georges Pompidou Museum in Paris in 1984. Vava had arranged a private meeting for me with Chagall at the museum two days before the official opening of the exhibition.

The museum guard escorted me to the rooms where the exhibition was shown, and there I saw Vava and Chagall standing in front of one of his fabulous ink drawings, which they were studying with great intensity. I clearly remember the peace and quiet of the room. It was the only time I was in a museum gallery with two other people.

Turning to me, Chagall said, "Seeing one of my drawings that I have not seen in a very long time is like seeing an old friend." He was so sincere about this meeting of himself, the artist, and his drawing. His memory of his relationship with the artwork was profound.

Every time I see someone that I have not seen in a long time, I think about Chagall on that afternoon, and the wonderful passionate relationship he had with his work. The message that I received that day is that we should pursue our passions in life and that passion will become our friend.

In Chagall's lifetime he suffered many personal setbacks. For example, he lived under, was persecuted by, and had to flee from, harsh dictatorships. In the 1920s, he had his paintings stolen in France and Germany. In 1944, he had to endure the loss of his first wife Bella. Yet, Chagall kept on working, and this is one of his messages – to find that ray of hope, and to never give up.

Chagall was a very prolific, industrious person. By the time you and I awaken in the morning and put on a pot of coffee, Chagall had probably sketched out his ideas for that day's work and had been at his easel for a few hours.

In a documentary produced by Chuck Olin, *"The Monumental Art of Marc Chagall,"* the artist was quoted. He spoke in French, "Travail, travail, travail, sans le travail on meurt." (Work, work, work, without work one dies). Yet Chagall's ideas and themes were not all that complex. He only worked to please himself, and by doing so, he pleased others with his creations.

After achieving fame from his oil paintings, it was in the last forty years of Chagall's life that he began to explore new paths of creativity. Hence, one of his most important messages is to constantly consider the undertaking of new and different forms of creative endeavor. This takes an open mind and an open heart.

In his case, he expanded his horizons in later years by working with ceramics, tapestry, stained glass windows, mosaics, lithographs, sculptures, and costume and set designs for theater and ballet. Vava inspired and encouraged him to take on large artistic projects. Among them were the decoration of the ceiling of the Paris Opera, the murals for New York's Metropolitan Opera and the windows for the St. Stephan Church in Mainz, Germany

Not only did Chagall explore various forms of art, but he also investigated other religions, incorporating other beliefs, symbols or icons in his art work. For instance, the Christ configuration of the crucifixion and resurrection shows that while he came from a strict Hasidic background, he was able to integrate Christ in his art work – a symbol of suffering for all humanity – thus bringing Christians together with other religions of the world.

Chagall also demonstrated that if you are in good health, mentally and physically, you can and should continue to contribute to a better world. The most productive years of his life were his last forty. Blessed with good health and vitality, he kept on creating great art into his ninety-seventh year. On the day he died, he had been working in his studio.

This message of Chagall was that of course you grow older, but you don't have to become old. His doctor told me, on the occasion of his 95th birthday party, that Chagall was so healthy, he would probably still be able to come and celebrate my 95th birthday with me. At the time, I was 47 years old!

One of the other messages that Chagall so thoroughly expresses is his ability to work with others to achieve some of his most outstanding artistic projects. The lesson learned from him is to have trust and confidence in the people you choose to work with you in the mediums that you cannot carry out by yourself.

Chagall was an absolute genius in getting others to do for him what he was unable to do for himself. For instance, he could not go out and raise funds for his Museum, but I could. I became one of his angels, accomplishing what he wanted done. He couldn't actually install a stained glass window, or weave a tapestry, or produce a mosaic. But he was a mastermind at choosing the right artisans who could work with him and who understood his gifts and could carry out his plans.

Chagall created the maquette, (the artistic sketches) for his stained glass windows, for the tapestries and the mosaics, but it was the great talent of artisans like Charles Marq, Yvette Cauquil-Prince, Michel Tharin, Lino Milano and others that brought Chagall's artwork into the new mediums. Chagall had the ability to win from his collaborators an absolute sense of loyalty and insight.

His favorite statement to his artisans was "Vous comprenez Chagall!" He chose only those who understood him, his goals, his aspirations and where he wanted to go. He maintained a steadfast input into every detail of his artistic creations, making each Chagall project a true Chagall. In collaborating with him, the artisan had to take a giant step backwards, overlaying his or her own talent with a precise interpretation of the Chagall style.

An utter perfectionist, Chagall insisted on preserving the highest standards for each and every element pertaining to his work. For instance, the quality of canvas or paper, the type of paints, the style of a font to be used on a poster had to measure up to his conception of excellence.

I learned early on in my working relationship with Chagall how imperative it was to meet his precise standards. I realized how detailed he was in his work, and how he labored over and over on a piece of art until he was completely satisfied that it reflected the peak of perfection

This concentration on never accepting anything but the absolute best became my benchmark as I dealt with a whole range of professional people on behalf of Chagall, and even as I prepared my lectures. When lecturing, I want the listener to hear the voice of Marc Chagall as if he himself were speaking.

An example of my focus on Chagall's message of total perfection took place in 2002, when at my urging, the Sandhills Jewish Congregation sponsored a "Chagall in Pinehurst" project as a fund-raiser. The weekend-long event included a piano recital, a children's program, related program activities and the sale of Chagall posters. A lecture was given by Bella Meyer, Chagall's granddaughter.

I received permission from the Artists Rights Society in New York to reproduce a portrayal of the love story of the Biblical characters of David and Bathsheba for the poster. Done in various shades of blue and white with a bouquet of flowers and scenes of Paris, angels and birds, it was a typical Chagall work. I took the reproduction to the printer who was doing the invitations for the event, but because of the complexity of the colors, the pixels would not work through his computer and printer. It looked awful.

Of course there were print shops in Raleigh that could handle the job. However, because of the distance involved, I wanted to find someone closer to do the work, and was fortunate to locate Kim Gilley, the owner of a superb and highly recommended local print shop. I told her I needed perfection, and she asked me to give her a week.

Unfortunately, the detail of color didn't meet what I knew in my heart was the Chagall standard. I explained it to her this way. "Imagine Marc Chagall is standing to my right. Your attempts with this project have not reached his demands of perfection." So Kim tried again to see if she could reproduce the details for the poster according to what I thought were the specifications of the artist.

After several unsuccessful attempts, Kim called to say that she had created a reproduction that she felt Chagall would like, and would I please come to the shop and see it. She met me at the counter, and unrolled the poster not in front of me, but to my right, saying, "Chagall, I hope you approve of this poster because it is the best that I can do."

I stood there looking at the poster, and had an imaginary conversation with Chagall, all the while that Kim held up the poster. I turned to Kim, and said, "Chagall approves. Print the poster."

Tracing the movements in the artistic world of the late 19th and early 20th century world of art, you can find "isms": modernism, naturalism, expressionism, symbolism, neoclassicism, romanticism, realism, pointillism, cubism, primitivism, suprematicism, fauvism, surrealism, to name the more important styles.

At the time Chagall was creating his artwork in Russia, the art world emerged with two new forms: social realism and constructivism. However, he resisted being classified as a proponent of any of the current "isms". In the face of poverty and during the very cold winters when there wasn't enough food, he never gave in to the other forms of Russian art.

When living in France, Chagall wrote, "I am not a reactionary from cubism. I have admired the great cubists and have profited from cubism. But... cubism seemed to limit pictorial expression unduly. To persist in that I felt was to impoverish one's vocabulary...I felt painting needed a greater freedom than cubism permitted. I felt somewhat justified later when I saw a swing toward expressionism in Germany and still more so when I saw the birth of surrealism in the early twenties. But I have always been against the idea of schools... explaining, "One must quench the richness of colour with one's soul."

He continued throughout his life to be unique in his style – there was only one Chagall. He stood alone, and he lived that message – you don't have to be like everyone else in order to succeed. Just do what your heart tells you. Do it with a firm commitment, and you will reach out to the world around you.

In describing the messages of Chagall, I have used the words "hope, peace, reconciliation and love." These are my words, not those of Chagall. However, having known him personally, and having been honored to have his friendship, and through voluminous study of his artwork and the books that have been written about him, I feel and know in my heart that this is the most important message that he has given, and keeps on giving, to the world.

Chapter 4
Musée National Message Biblique Marc Chagall

Marc Chagall's finest bequest lives on in his Biblical Message Museum in Nice, France. To understand Chagall's fascination with the Bible and its powerful influence on his work, what better way to appreciate its meaning than to let him speak for himself. The museum is now known as the Musée National Marc Chagall.

Chagall wrote, "I went back to the great universal book, the Bible. Since my childhood, it has filled me with vision about the fate of the world and inspired me in my work. In moments of doubt, its highly poetic grandeur and wisdom have comforted me. For me it is like a second nature. I see the events of life and works of art through the wisdom of the Bible - a truly great work penetrated by its spirit and harmony...Since in my inner life the spirit and world of the Bible occupy a large place, I have tried to express it (through my work)."

Chagall's Biblical art is strongly rooted in the village of his childhood, Vitebsk, Belarus. Yet the spirit of his characters of the Bible, portraying the faces of the matriarchs and patriarchs of his Russian birthplace, can be seen in the faces of Abraham, Isaac, Jacob and Moses. One can imagine Chagall sitting in the Jewish school reading the Bible and transferring every day images to the Biblical stories.

Through the efforts of André Malraux, the Deputy Minister of Culture under Charles de Gaulle, the artist's dream of a place to assemble his works in a museum devoted to the Bible became a reality. Malraux, who became united emotionally and intellectually with Chagall on the completion of this project, is known for his comment, "If we don't have spirituality in the 20th century, we will not have a 21st century."

At first, the government offered Chagall an old 17th century chapel in Chemin du Calvaire as a place to assemble his works, an ensemble of his paintings of the Biblical message. He ultimately rejected the site because of its shape and small dimensions. However, it was also much too humid a place to hang the canvases. Another reason for the rejection was that while the chapel was owned by the town, the Catholic Church still had the right to hold Mass there. Chagall commented, "I didn't want...any ties with formal dogma – Catholic, Jewish or any other kind. I just wanted to create an atmosphere for meditation and spiritual peace."

A piece of land was found close to Chagall's home near Nice, in the hills of Cimiez. The architect, André Hermant, captured the poignant and spiritual feelings of Chagall in the design of the structure. As conceived by Hermant, the architecture shows the lightness and colors of Chagall's art at their best through the sobriety of the walls and the strictness of form.

The handsome Museum, surrounded by a pool and a garden, was dedicated on Chagall's birthday, July 7, 1973, with artwork donated by Marc and Valentina (Vava) Chagall. The focal point of the Museum is the seventeen major paintings done by Chagall from 1954-1957, depicting the biblical stories of *Genesis, Exodus* and the *Song of Songs*.

Eventually, the Chagalls donated sketches and drawings that were the preparatory work Chagall had done for the seventeen paintings. Also among the 450 Chagall works in the collection are pastels and oil paintings, gouaches, lithographs and sculptures, ceramics, a mosaic, three stained glass windows based on the creation of the world and a tapestry.

Fundamental to the theme of the Biblical Message Museum was Chagall's insistence on the inclusion of all the religions of the world. The permanent exhibitions are based on the Old Testament while the temporary exhibitions reflect religious art and special Chagall exhibitions. The museum's library also contains a combination of art books and materials on diverse religions.

Chagall was determined that his Museum be a sanctuary of peace for all people. An apt description of what Chagall wished to accomplish with his Museum is found in the words of a Hebrew poet, Abba Kovner, "To remember the past, To live the present, To trust the future."

In a rare interview with Carlton Lake of *The Atlantic* that appeared in a July 1963 issue, Chagall explained that the seventeen paintings that were originally donated to the museum "form an army when they're together. But if they were scattered here and there, they're just individual soldiers. You can't win that way. I'm against museums. But a message, one can leave. If these things have value, they'll create their own museum."

Chagall was the only living artist in the late 1960s and early 1970s that had his own museum. Later on when other museums were built featuring work of artists like Picasso and Leger, what disturbed Chagall was that his Biblical Message Museum didn't draw the numbers of people that the Picasso museums in Paris and Antibes attracted. At that time there were thirty-four nationalized art museums in France under the Ministry of Culture, including both the Chagall and Picasso museums.

In addition to Chagall's great artistic talent, he had excellent marketing and public relations instincts. He conceived a plan for reaching out to the American public to encourage them to come and visit his museum in Nice. With the assistance of Eleanor Wood-Prince of Chicago, The American Friends of the Chagall Biblical Message Museum, an association, was formed, similar to the one that was already in place in France.

Founded in 1976, the American Friends' mission was to "cultivate, promote, foster and develop the appreciation, taste and love of the Biblical Message Museum and other artistic works of Marc Chagall," and "to secure the interest and support of patrons of the arts." Fund-raising projects were undertaken during the ensuing years to accomplish successfully the goals of the American Friends' mission.

Mrs. Wood-Prince figured prominently in the achievement of these objectives through her superlative contacts with important officials in the French government and with renowned art collectors both in the United States and abroad. One of the unique programs in which her contacts played an important role was the issuance of a special admissions card to any French national museum.

The cards were given to those people who bought a signed Chagall poster for $1,000 entitling the purchasers to membership in the American Friends of the Biblical Message Museum. The cards were very attractive and decorated with a little Chagall angel.

One very hot July day in 1982, when Ralph and I were in Paris, we decided to go the Versailles Palace. It was, of course, at the height of the tourist season, and the lines were very long. I told Ralph to hold our place in line while I went to see if my card would do us any good. I walked about a block and half to the main entrance, and spoke to a woman who was in charge of admissions. I showed her my card, and received an immediate and very cordial response.

The woman asked me to have a seat on a yellow velvet settee which I am sure belonged to Louis XIV, while she made arrangements for me to be admitted. When I explained that my husband was waiting in line, I was told to go and find him so that we could be included in the next group with an English speaking guide. Despite Ralph's embarrassment as we walked past hundreds of tourists from countries around the globe who were patiently waiting in line, we were admitted to Versailles within a very few minutes.

All because of this little Chagall card, Ralph says, "What a buy!" And it's unbelievable when I consider the hours I haven't had to spend standing in line at exhibitions at some of the finest French art museums, not counting all the complimentary admission charges.

As part of the plan to motivate American art patrons to become familiar with, and to gain financial support for the Museum and the works of Chagall, I would plan trips to France and other locations in Europe, as well as trips to Israel to see the stained glass windows at the Hadassah Hospital in Jerusalem and other artwork. Sometimes these trips would feature visits with the Chagalls at their home, or to private art collections or special events such as luncheons, receptions or dinner parties, again arranged through Eleanor Wood-Prince.

One such occasion was a fabulous dinner party given by Gérald Van der Kemp, the conservateur of the Versailles Palace, and his wife, Florence. What an unbelievable evening!

The couple lived in the apartments of the Palace that were originally built for Colbert, the Minister of Finance for Louis XIV. At the time the Van der Kemps were very involved with trying to raise funds for the restoration of Giverney, Monet's home, and were happy to welcome a group of American art patrons.

There were eighteen of us in the group, including Mrs. Wood-Prince's attorney, Thomas Tyler, a tall, distinguished looking gentleman. On the afternoon preceding the dinner, he informed me that he was not going to the dinner because an important legal matter demanded his attention in Chicago on the following day.

I called Madame Van der Kemp and apologized to her, saying that we would be seventeen, not eighteen. I had the unmistakable feeling she was a bit annoyed. About a half hour later, Mr. Tyler phoned, telling me that he had made arrangements for his law partner to handle the matter for him, and that he would be delighted to attend the dinner.

So once more I telephoned Madame Van der Kemp and with many apologies, explained that the plans had changed, and that our number would be eighteen after all. To which she replied, "You are either going to be seventeen or eighteen. Which is it? This is a very big dinner, with fifty-two guests, and I have invited the most important people in France in honor of the American Friends of the Chagall Museum. I am not going to let you upset my plans and make last minute changes. So you had better decide on your numbers!"

I told her that the final number would be eighteen, and hung up the phone, absolutely shattered by her grave concern. I rushed out of my room in tears, and was standing in the hallway, when a member of our group found me and wanted to know what the problem was. I told him the story and questioned what I would do if Mr. Tyler changed his mind another time and couldn't show up for the dinner.

As a man of good humor, he quieted me by stating that the doorman at the Ritz Hotel on the Place Vendome where we were staying was a look-alike for Mr. Tyler. "If necessary, I and the other men in the group will kidnap the doorman, strip him of his uniform and dress him in Mr. Tyler's tuxedo, shove him into the limousine and pass him off as Mr. Tyler." By the time he finished giving me the details about pulling off this scenario, I went from crying my heart out to laughing uncontrollably.

Needless to say, all eighteen of our group arrived at the Versailles Palace, and upon our arrival, I understood why Florence Van der Kemp had been so upset about my two phone calls. There I saw a huge board painted in watercolors, sitting on a easel, a fantastic seating chart that was a work of art, with numbered circles and names written in beautiful calligraphy. Obviously the arrangement had to be changed with each phone call.

At first, I didn't see my name, and for a moment thought that I was excluded because of the trouble I had caused. Just at that moment, Florence Van der Kemp rushed up to me. "Vivian, you have to do me a huge favor, please say yes. You must host the table in the small dining room. We have more people than can be seated in the main dining room, so we are using the small dining room as well, and I need you to be the hostess."

The walls of the "small" dining room (actually a huge room) were hung with forest green silk peau de soie, and the room was delicately lit with crystal chandeliers and sterling silver candelabras. Among the twelve guests in the small dining room, to my right was the editor of the *Paris Match* and to my left was an executive of the Banque National de Paris. Seated across from me, but at opposite ends of the table, were a man and a woman from England whom hadn't seen each other for years. They were prominent actors, now in their late 70's, who had great difficulties conversing over the guest seated between them.

I decided to cure the unforeseen situation, so as hostess, I recommended a seating change so that this couple could sit together. My suggestion was accepted among gales of laughter from the other guests, who had never taken part in such a novel seating rearrangement in the midst of a formal dinner party.

And the editor of *Paris Match* had the last word. "Only the women's liberation movement in America would produce a woman that could change the seating arrangement at a dinner party given by Florence Van der Kemp!"

As I was saying my goodbyes to Madame Van der Kemp, thanking her for a lovely evening, she gave me a friendly slap on the back, and said, "Forget all that formality, Vivian. We're just happy to have you here." I learned later that she was a native Texan, who went to school in Switzerland before meeting her husband and becoming the wife of the director of the Versailles Palace.

Another very special occasion awaited the group in Cannes. Once again, through connections of Eleanor Wood-Prince, we received an invitation for a luncheon at the home of Florence Gould, a patron of the arts, and the daughter of a French publisher who made his fortune in the United States. She had interrupted her career as an opera singer when she married the son of Jay Gould, the American railroad magnate.

Widowed in 1956, Madame Gould had one of the largest private collections of Impressionist art in her three story home overlooking the Mediterranean Sea. And she had arranged to have Daniel Wildenstein, a prominent French art dealer, flown from Paris to Cannes so that our group would have an authentic introduction to the Gould collection.

Eleanor asked me to call Florence Gould to accept her gracious invitation, and gave me the telephone number. The only problem was that we had previously pre-ordered and given a deposit for lunch at one of Cannes' most famous hotels.

I called and introduced myself to Madame Gould and explained why we would have to decline the invitation. She replied in a very commanding voice, "You are coming to my house for lunch and Daniel Wildenstein, my art dealer from Paris will join us. You are a total of eighteen, and I have twenty-two servants, so it is not a problem for me. Just call the hotel in Cannes and tell them that you are coming to my house for lunch." Formidable – yes! Scary – definitely!

When I called the maitre d' at the hotel to cancel, he was furious beyond words, and reminded me that we had already given a 50% deposit. "You can keep the deposit," I said. Finally, he asked in chilled tones, "May I inquire at what restaurant you are going to be dining?" To which I replied, "We have been invited to the home of Florence Gould."

Complete silence. Then he said, very politely, "Of course, I understand, and we will return the deposit. I hear that her home is lovely with a superb art collection. You are most fortunate to have received such a magnificent invitation." The deposit check was received in the United States two weeks later.

My memory of that day and the wonderful luncheon is a special one. We felt as if we were entering the Pentagon because of the security inspection of our passports and other identification that we encountered upon arrival. As I glanced around the spacious interior of the home, I saw works of Renoir, Degas, Cezanne, Pissarro, and a room solely with Bonnard paintings.

The sun shone into the house from the Mediterranean Sea, and as we wandered, viewing the splendid collection, Wildenstein would give a brilliant scholarly dissertation of each painting. A stack of art books on a table in a small room facing the sea was a testament to Florence Gould's avid interest in art, and to her intelligent approach to her constant acquisition of new works.

A week later I flew from Nice to Paris. My seat mate was the mayor of Cannes, who had served in that position for many years. I introduced myself as President of the American Friends of Chagall's Biblical Message Museum, and during our conversation, mentioned that our group had had lunch and a private tour at the home of Florence Gould. He was stunned, advising me that that in all the years he had been mayor of the city he had never been invited to her home. "You and your group of Friends must be very special people."

On another journey when I escorted a party of benefactors to Nice to become acquainted with all aspects of the Biblical Message Museum and to view Chagall's artworks on display, we were again accompanied by Eleanor Wood-Prince. One of the luxurious residences we visited where we were guests at a festive cocktail party belonged to Mr. and Mrs. William Hagerty, whose family corporation was the well known maker of silver polish. We were welcomed most graciously to their gorgeous 17th floor apartment in Monaco, overlooking the Mediterranean coastline, where a beautiful Chagall oil painting portraying a lush bouquet of flowers hung in the foyer.

At the cocktail party Eleanor decided to invite some new people whom she had recently met to join us for dinner the following evening, and later asked me to take care of the details of including them in our group at the Hotel De Paris. As the menu was already chosen for the sixteen people in our party, I had to figure out how to provide for four more guests.

I met with the chef of the famed restaurant the next morning to discuss the problem. He was very perturbed, since the food and wines had previously been ordered. He cared less about who invited the extra people; it was his kitchen, and his preparation was all that mattered. When I suggested that the soup, medallions of veal, vegetables and dessert could be divided up to serve an additional four people, he looked at me with an air of disbelief.

Although I had not learned the technique of what to do to stretch the food to feed extra guests from my mother, I did learn it at camp. As a junior counselor, I was put in charge of an outdoor cookout deep in the Wisconsin woods.

While building the campfire, the head counselor informed me that there would be ten extra people that had to be fed, and showed me how to divide up the food so that no one would know the difference. It was that same lesson learned when I was fifteen that I used with the chef in the kitchen at the Hotel de Paris in Monaco. I left him shaking his head, and I could hear him saying to himself "These American women!"

Feeling full of chutzpah as I exited the kitchen, I observed the orchestra leader in the dining room looking over the dinner music that was planned for the evening. Introducing myself as the president of the Chagall association in the United States, I told him that a group of us would be having dinner in the dining room that night.

I asked him if the orchestra knew the song, *"Chicago, That Toddling Town,"* and if so, would they please play it when our group entered the dining room. "No problem," was his reply.

At precisely 8 p.m., we walked into the dining room, and I gave the orchestra leader a hand signal. We marched to our table, led by Eleanor, to the strains of a lively rendition of *"Chicago",* laughing and singing all the way. The other guests in the room were completely taken aback by such a raucous entry, but the American Friends of the Chagall Biblical Message Museum showed their pride and love for their home city a half a world away that night at the Hotel de Paris in Monaco.

Chapter 5
The Harpsichord

When the plans were being drawn for the Musée National Message Biblique, Chagall was unwavering in his decision that the structure should contain a concert hall. A lover of classical music and the scenic arts, he firmly believed that the integration of art and music was an important facet of bringing peace to mankind, and overrode any objections to include a 300 seat auditorium as a fundamental part of his museum.

Chagall drew the designs for three stained glass windows, illustrating *The Creation of the World*, which bathed the auditorium in an exceptional blue light, and from the beginning the stage contained a magnificent grand piano. This concert hall would eventually host recitals for some of the greatest musicians of the 20th century.

Among them have been pianists Alicia de Larrocha and Vladimir Ashkenazy, and sopranos Victoria de los Angeles and Elly Ameling. The noted violinist Yehudi Menuhin, appeared on the stage at the museum, as well as Chagall's friend, cellist Mstislav Rostropovitch. Ensembles such as the Beaux Arts Trio, the Mozarteum Quartet and the Academy of St. Martin in the Field have also brought the gift of music to the museum.

Several years after the opening of the museum, on a trip to Paris when Chagall and Vava were strolling along one of the famous boulevards, his eye caught an antique harpsichord on display in a shop window. What a beautiful addition a harpsichord would make for the concert hall at the museum!

To accomplish the task of securing such an instrument and raising the funds to purchase it, he turned to the American Friends of the Biblical Message Museum. The plan as conceived by Chagall and Vava, together with the director of the Museum, Pierre Provoyeur, and with the approval of Eleanor Wood-Prince, was to have an 18th century French Blanchet harpsichord replicated at a cost of approximately $25,000.

The funds needed for the project would come from the sale of signed Chagall posters. To reinforce the authenticity of the posters, each one would bear what was called an imprimé - a small, embossed Chagall angel holding a menorah.

My part in the plan, as president of the American association of the Museum, was to go to Nice, visit with Chagall, pick up the signed posters, and then embark on a promotional tour to acquaint audiences with the museum and sell the posters   The tour proved to be enormously successful.

Armed with a slide show presentation on the seventeen major Biblical paintings in the museum, I lectured in Los Angeles at an art gallery, and in Florida spoke at the opening of a shopping mall. I gave lectures in Chicago (one for the Alliance Française in French), in New York, Milwaukee and in Washington, D.C. I raised much more than the $25,000 in no time. People loved Chagall! They were more than willing to purchase signed posters, that sold for between $500 and $1500.

In all the prior planning, however, no one had thought of how we were going export signed Chagall posters with the distinctive imprimé out of France. Would the French customs and security knowingly permit more than fifty valuable posters to leave their country? Absolutely not!

And not so surprisingly, it fell into my hands to save the day.

Somewhere in the vaults of the basement of the museum, Pierre Provoyeur and his staff found a large cardboard tube, which resembled a bazooka gun. Each of the fifty-two signed posters was clad in several layers of tissue paper, and rolled very tightly before being placed in the tube. I was to carry the tube on the plane with me, and if stopped by a French official, I was instructed to say the tube carried a gift for my husband.

I asked a question about insurance, but was told there could be no insurance because then a report would have to be made to the Beaux Arts Committee in Paris, so I flew from Nice to Paris and across the Atlantic carrying the unwieldy package by hand. Twice I was questioned by authorities about its contents, and twice I innocently replied, "Just a gift for my husband."

I was a nervous wreck. After all I was carrying over $50,000 worth of posters with no insurance. The biggest problem came when the plane landed in New York, hours late due to a violent thunderstorm which caused me to miss my connecting flight to Chicago. I was shuttled to a small inferior hotel for an overnight stay before my flight the following morning.

My room had very dark walls, not too much lighting, a bathroom that I didn't want to use, and a security system at the door that was zero on a scale of one to ten. Forget the amenities – the question was the security of my "bazooka gun."

Then a childhood experience popped into my head. When I was at summer camp, and we wanted to escape the cabin after lights out, we would create a human form from a sleeping bag to fool the flashlight-bearing counselors checking on their charges. We became experts at faking sleeping campers.

Inspired by this idea, I rolled the large tube into two blankets and propped it up on a pillow. I fell asleep, hugging 'Ralph' and asking God to watch over me and the posters.

Needless to say, I and my hand-held luggage arrived safely the next day, and a home was found for the posters in the vaults of the Northern Trust Bank. About three weeks later, Eleanor Wood-Prince informed me that a terrible mistake had been discovered.

Someone at the Museum had neglected to place the imprimé on the posters before sending them off in my care. She could tell by the look on my face that there was no way I was going back to France with the posters, and then make the return trip a second time. She found a courier and in less than a week the posters with the imprimé were back in the Northern Trust vault.

Meanwhile, the harpsichord under careful construction in Paris at the Atelier William Dowd. The instrument was actually built by Dowd's very talented partner Reinhard von Nagel, a most charming man of German origin, who spoke French and English fluently. It was von Nagel's idea to have Chagall paint the inside cover of the harpsichord with a Biblical scene.

Painted musical instruments, such as harpsichords and the viola de gamba, were commonplace in the 17th and 18th centuries. However, in the 20th century an artist of the stature of Marc Chagall had never painted a "couvercle" of a harpsichord. Chagall's mind and spirit were excited by von Nagel's suggestion, particularly since music was so much a part of his life.

Chagall chose the love story of Isaac and Rebecca, and created from his heart and his hand a painting that depicts the couple at the well, with their matchmaker Eliezer in the background. The painting also shows the tree of life, and the city of Jerusalem embellished by King David and other Chagall symbols.

The delicate construction of the harpsichord proceeded on schedule, and Chagall completed his work on the painting. At this time, the museum contacted me. They wanted to have an inscription lettered in gold on the instrument. The suggestion for the French wording is translated here into English: *This harpsichord whose cover was graciously painted by Marc Chagall was donated by the Association of the American Friends of the Chagall Biblical Message Museum – Chicago, Illinois, January 4, 1981.*

I was pleased with the wording which was then sent to Hubert Landais, the Minister of Culture of France, for his approval. It turned out, however, that he wanted the words "Chicago, Illinois" deleted. I was furious! For a woman who was born and raised in Chicago, the city that produced the Cubs, the White Sox, Bears and Blackhawks, and a city that was the home of the American Friends, there was no way that Monsieur Landais could have his way.

I recalled when Madame Gérald Van der Kemp was the president of the American Friends of Versailles Palace, she had headed the fundraising for a Steinway grand piano, which bore the inscription: *This piano was given by the American Friends of Versailles Palace (New York, New York)* If New York, New York was inscribed on the Versailles piano, Chicago, Illinois could be put on the Musée Chagall harpsichord. When this was pointed out to Monsieur Landais, he relented and the inscription remained in its original form.

The day was approaching when I would have to sit down and start writing my speech for the dedication of the harpsichord. The money had been raised, the instrument was completed, the date and time for the dedication set, and Pierre Provoyeur, the museum's director, had honored me by asking that I give the dedication speech. I had three months to think about what I wanted to say before the more than three hundred invited guests, including distinguished French officials.

I kept thinking over Chagall's idea of the integration of art and music producing peace. Somewhere in my experience as a child or an adult, there was a linkage, but what was the source? Then one day while standing at my kitchen sink, God blessed me with a remembrance of a long ago summer afternoon.

I was twelve years old, and walking in the late afternoon sunset towards my camp cabin after swimming at the waterfront. I heard this beautiful piano music coming from the social hall, and an unseen force drew me into the building. Brothers Alex and Jonathan Goldstein, both counselors, were seated next to each other at an old rickety upright piano playing beautifully. They told me later the piece was a Beethoven sonata for four hands that their mother had taught them.

While they were playing, another dynamic counselor, Yochanan Muffs, was painting a mural on a long sheet of brown wrapping paper with bright colors of orange and yellow. The scene was to be the backdrop for a play on the story of Jonah. I sat on a green bench in my wet bathing suit, a bathing cap still on my head, a towel draped around my shoulders and quietly listened.

I must have felt something very extraordinary and spiritual about the combination of the arts displayed that afternoon, because it was this powerful experience – the beauty of art and music taking place at the same time – that became the foundation for my dedication speech for the Chagall harpsichord.

I wanted to give not only a good speech, but a great one. I had to give the speech in French, and I wanted to show the French officials who would attend the ceremony that Americans are a cultured people, who can speak their language properly. After writing five drafts of the speech, I took it to my French teacher, at Northeastern Illinois University, Dr. Dorette Klein, who helped me to perfect it, and who coached me in the days leading up to the dedication.

A Ph.D. graduate from DePaul University in music and piano, who had taken post graduate studies at the University of Chicago, Dr. Klein was born and raised in France. She insisted on fluent French from her students, along with the right intonation and musicality which the language demands of its speaker. While I spoke Hebrew in the accent of north side Chicago, my French was at that time straight out of Paris.

In my dedication speech, I said, in part, "The artist, musician and poet express the ultimate ideals of a dream. People who live with the reality of problems and complexities of the world try to incorporate the ideas of the artist in their daily lives. The arts bring together people with different traditions, cultures, heritages and religious beliefs in an environment of understanding and the hope for peace…"

Then I included a quotation from Genesis, Chapter 24, verse 67 about the meeting and marriage of Isaac and Rebecca. It was purposely given in Hebrew, and I then continued with the French translation.

"Then Isaac brought her into the tent, and took Rebecca, and she became his wife, and he loved her..."

This was my answer to the anti-Semitism, which had resulted in an attack on October 3, 1980 on a Jewish synagogue in Paris during the High Holy Days the previous year.

And I finished my remarks by saying, once again in French, "May the message of eternal love of Isaac and Rebecca so wondrously painted by Marc Chagall and the sounds of music that will come forth from this harpsichord continue to inspire beauty and understanding and peace throughout the world."

The official dedication ceremony took place on January 4, 1981, at 5 p.m. Gustav Leonhardt, the world renowned harpsichordist from Amsterdam, was engaged to present a concert of Couperin, Rameau and Bach. The demand for tickets to the concert was so great that another concert was added at 11 a.m.

My speech was received very warmly, with many compliments on my pronunciation, fluency and diction. A writer for the *Nice Matin* newspaper gave Leonhardt a brilliant and elegantly worded review of his passionate playing, and several international publications published write-ups or photos of this important event in the art world.

The story of the occasion wouldn't be complete, however, without a recounting of what I wore on that momentous day. As the time grew closer to the day of the dedication, I was so consumed with my speech and with my French professor, that I hadn't given a thought to what I was going to wear.

Everyone who was ever associated with Chagall, his family, friends and colleagues, would be in the audience, and I wanted to wear something special and appropriate. Like every woman in the moment of such a crisis, I opened my closet and realized that I didn't have a thing to wear.

My solution to the problem was to head straight for Loehmann's, Chicago's famous markdown clothing store. I chose this store because it would be the quickest one to enter and exit and not get caught in a rush hour jam. Not wanting to waste a minute, I took a Transit Authority bus and train transfer for the grand sum of $1.25 that would be good for a two hour period.

Entering the store, I quickly began looking for a dress or suit. A very lovely slim salesperson approached me and asked if she could help me. When I told her I wanted something for a very special occasion, she asked if it was for a wedding, anniversary, bar mitzvah, or some other celebration. Remembering the time-stamped transfer in my pocket, I went right to the point.

"Actually I am leaving in forty-eight hours for Nice, France, where I am going to give a speech," and then rapidly described for her every single detail of the dedication ceremony I was going to be attending. She replied, "I have just the outfit for you. You are a size 16, correct?"

I was so confident that she indeed would have the perfect outfit, that I promptly entered the dressing room and started to disrobe. When she returned, she was holding a Harvé Benard maroon velvet suit with a high collar, no buttons, puff sleeves - very 18th century in look - and a knee length straight skirt. It fitted perfectly. Next she brought in a rose pink silk blouse, and VOILA, there was the Chagall harpsichord dedication outfit.

Looking at myself in the mirror, I was stunned that this all happened so quickly, and that actually I was going to make it back home using my transfer. As I was dressing I thought that this woman was a true Chagall angel. I paid for my purchases and left the store a very happy woman.

At the dedication, many pictures were taken. However, the one that is my favorite was taken in the evening when I visited Chagall at La Colline, his home in St. Paul de Vence. He hadn't attended the actual ceremony, and I presented my speech to him personally. The picture shows the two of us going over the speech and discussing it in French and Yiddish.

Chagall looked at me after reading the speech and holding my hand, he said "Vous comprenez Chagall!" He approved of my words regarding his message of love, peace and understanding. I was thrilled with his comment.

A month after I returned home I had the picture duplicated and sent it to the president of Loehmann's, telling him the story about the all time perfect salesperson that served me so well. I also went back to the store to find her and give her a copy of the picture.

Much to my great disappointment, I was informed that she had moved on to Bloomingdale's in New York to direct one of their departments. Little did she ever know the joy she brought into my life that January day!

Chapter 6
Reconciliation

The words that I spoke during the dedication of the Blanchet harpsichord, "The arts bring together people with different traditions, cultures, heritages and religious beliefs in an environment of understanding and the hope for peace…" were, in fact, in the process of becoming reality even as I delivered them. Chagall was in the midst of his creation of the glorious stained glass windows at St. Stephan Catholic Church in Mainz, Germany. The magnificent windows based on the Old Testament characters and a Christ configuration of the resurrection were a continuing project for Chagall spanning the years from 1976 to 1984. This proved to be a sublime example of the artist's concern for humanity, and one which deeply affected me and my husband.

The historic church of St. Stephan, founded in 990 A.D., was almost completely devastated during World War II, but slowly it was restored. In the spring of 1973, the Pfarrer (parish priest) at the church, Klaus Mayer, approached Chagall, whom he called "the master of colour and the Biblical message" with the idea of creating stained glass windows for the apse of the rebuilt structure.

According to Mayer, it took more than three years of letter writing and meetings to persuade Chagall to agree to consider the project. "Chagall's decision to do the windows was extremely difficult. After the war, he didn't want anything to do with Germany. I had to keep reminding him how important it was to make a visible contribution in the silent language of stained glass."

Finally, Chagall started work on the sketches in 1976. The stained glass windows were intended by him as an artistic symbol of the new friendship between France, his adopted country, and Germany, and a pledge of international understanding and a commitment to world peace. For Chagall, a Jewish artist, the St. Stephan windows were a commission of reconciliation between the two countries and two great religions; it was these magnificent windows that became an important and influential part of our marriage.

Ralph was born and spent the first eleven years of his life in Osnabrueck, Germany. His father, Dr. Ernst Jacobson, was a prominent attorney. After

Hitler came to power in 1933, his father, a Jew, was prohibited from practicing as a "notar," the highest ranking a lawyer could hold. Dr. Jacobson was forced to give up his partnership with a Christian partner, and soon after, two uniformed SS men were stationed at his office for many weeks to discourage clients from retaining him.

Other signs of anti-Semitism became increasingly prevalent in the following years. Prior to 1933 the family had Christian as well as Jewish friends, but after Hitler's election, Ralph was forbidden to play with or talk to his best friend, Wolfgang Kreft, the son of an important notar and attorney, who had apprenticed in his father's office.

Ralph and his sister, Elsa, who was four years older, were also barred from attending public school. Instead they received their education in a one-room school where one teacher taught children from the first through the eighth grades. The school building was next to a synagogue. In 1937, his sister turned fourteen and graduated from the school, and shortly thereafter she was fortunately allowed to emigrate to New York City to live with the family of an uncle.

By 1938, Jewish businesses had been confiscated. Signs had been posted "No Jews Allowed" in stores and public meeting places across the city.

On Saturday, October 8, 1938, Ralph went to synagogue services and his father went to the nearby family garden, hidden behind eight foot high hedges and protected by a heavy wooden gate. Ralph returned from services in the early afternoon as his mother was preparing lunch. She received a call to come to the hospital. An hour later she came home in tears and told Ralph that his father had passed away. When questioned, she stated quietly that he died of a heart attack. Dr. Jacobson was buried several days later in his family's cemetery in Hildesheim.

One month later Ralph and his mother experienced Kristallnacht or The Night of Crystal. That night synagogues all over Germany were demolished or severely damaged. In the middle of the night, four uniformed Nazi officers awakened Ralph's mother and ordered all occupants into the hallways. She told them that she was a widow, with a young son asleep. Ralph was called to the hallways while the men searched the home, purportedly looking for Jewish men. When they questioned Ralph's age and were told that he was ten, they said quickly, "That is too young" and left. Ralph and his mother could not understand the statement and wondered, too young for what?

Later that morning Ralph went to his school to find the school building and synagogue mostly demolished, with the sacred Torahs, prayer books and prayer shawls strewn in the street. Quickly running home, Ralph spoke of the damaged synagogue and his mother told him that all Jewish males in Osnabrueck over age fifteen had been arrested during the night, processed and taken to concentration camps. That answered our question, too young for what?

Ralph's parents had applied several years before to come to the United States. However, a quota dictated how many people would be allowed to enter from each country, a slow process with long waiting lists. After Kristallnacht Ralph could no longer attend school. Furthermore, it was dangerous to leave the house for any reason. Finally, the news came that Ralph and his mother could emigrate in January 1939, and they arrived in New York with very few belongings and assets of approximately $50.

Fast forward some fifty-four years later, when a book arrived in our Pinehurst mailbox. The book detailed the history of the Jewish community of Osnabrueck during the period of 1900–1945, co-written by Martina Sellmeyer Krause and Peter Junk.

When Ralph started reading the portion of the book devoted to his family's history, he became furious. I had never seen him so angry. The book reported that his father had committed suicide in October 1938. "This is not true," he persisted.

The next ten days were filled with dreadful questions, for which we had no answers. The tension occasioned by the account of his father's death was affecting our lives. Every waking minute was filled with shock and alarming thoughts.

What were the true circumstances surrounding Ralph's father's death? Why would his mother never speak about that terrible day? Ralph couldn't believe the official report of his death, but why and how had such a falsehood been manufactured?

Finally, an important decision was reached. We resolved to go to Osnabrueck to find the answers. Ralph was wary as to how he would be received, so we decided that I would go and question the intentions of the city to rectify what Ralph considered to be a grievous error.

I left for Germany in March 1994. We had agreed that my first stop would be in Mainz, to view the St. Stephan stained glass windows, and to talk about the reported suicide of Ralph's father with Father Mayer. Previously, we had met him at Chagall's 95th birthday party in the summer of 1982, and he had described for us the rich blue background, the Old Testament Biblical characters and the angelic forms that are portrayed in the windows.

At that time, the first three sections of the windows at St. Stephan were completed and installed in 1978, 1979, and 1981. Later in 1982, Chagall would draw the sketches for the fourth section of the windows – the great three-light windows in the transept of the church.

Now twelve years after first meeting Klaus Mayer, I experienced the beauty and the wonder of the Chagall windows in Mainz. As I entered the church, I realized it was unlike any other Catholic church I had ever visited. It was large, but very, very simple. As I faced the altar, I immediately was overcome by Chagall's message of peace and reconciliation between Germany and France and between Christians and Jews. My eyes were going from the vertical to the horizontal, trying to absorb everything in one captured moment. When I viewed the windows, I recalled how Chagall explained the art form:

"A stained glass window has a different fate from a painting. Because of the setting, the eye does not look at it in the same way as a collection of paintings. The eye of a man at prayer is simply part of his heart. For me a stained glass window is a transparent partition between my heart and the heart of the world. Stained glass has to be serious and passionate. It is something elevating and exhilarating. It has to live through the perception of light. To read the Bible is to perceive a certain light, and the window has to make this obvious through its simplicity and grace."

Hundreds of thousands of tourists from all over the world have made a pilgrimage to view the glowing stained glass windows in the austere setting of this church that had its beginnings over one thousand years ago. Could anyone deny that the blue light from the windows brings Chagall's angels and biblical characters to life?

I stayed to listen to one of Father Mayer's meditations. One and one-half hours in length, they are still being given at the time of the sixth printing of this book, and have reached over 3,780 in number. Statesmen from countries large and small have been among the many who have heard his presentation.

As Father Mayer gave his meditation, I thought about Chagall and this commission. Chagall had needed reconciliation in his own life and for his own experiences with the pogroms and anti-Semitism which he had suffered.

He had found it through the creation of the windows. And all of a sudden I realized in the depths of my heart that Ralph could have a similar reconciliation with Osnabrueck, Germany.

Upon arrival in Osnabrueck, I was greeted by the assistant to the mayor. The mayor, Hans Jürgen-Fip, had been most gracious and helpful in making arrangements for my stay. I toured the city with Peter Junk, and Martina Sellmeyer Krause gave me all the information that they had been able to locate about my father-in-law, the highly respected practicing lawyer, trustee and secretary for the Jewish congregation.

That night, I was numb with exhaustion. I turned to the material I received from Father Mayer in Mainz and was comforted by the references to the Book of Psalms that are so beautifully depicted in the windows.

I had left the United States with a very thin briefcase, and returned home after this very difficult trip with one that was bulging with letters, documents and photos. After Ralph had had an opportunity to sort through all the papers I had brought, he still did not have all the answers to his questions. Since he had been an attorney all his life, I suggested that the time had come for him to personally take up his father's defense, determine the real cause of his death, and clear his name.

After much discussion, I convinced him to take a trip to Osnabrueck the following year. In the meantime he would start building the case with whatever information was available from the documentation that I had gathered.

We would, of course, first visit Mainz to afford Ralph the opportunity to view the Chagall windows for himself. I felt it was important for us individually and for our marriage, for him to find the sense of peace and reconciliation which the windows have brought to all those who seen them.

Unfortunately, a few days before our planned trip to Germany, Ralph became ill, and we learned very quickly that he had to undergo heart surgery. The journey was put off for a year, and finally took place in March 1996.

Ralph was scheduled to speak at three of the schools in Osnabrueck about his experiences in the 1930s. Knowing that the students would ask disturbing questions of Ralph, I was glad that we had planned to stop in Mainz first.

After seeing the windows and listening to one of Father Mayer's meditations, Ralph told me that he found the whole experience very inspirational which gave him a feeling of peace.

As a result when the students asked him "Do you hate us?" he could truthfully answer, "How can I hate you? You didn't do anything to me. It is in the past, but we must never forget the Holocaust, and never let it happen again. It is difficult for me to accept what I believe to be the circumstances of my father's death. Yet I do forgive, and forgiveness is the first step to creating a new life and seeking peace."

As the years passed, we made five more trips to Germany, and each time Ralph's feeling of reconciliation deepened. The reconciliation reflected sadness, but it also contained a new beginning of happiness.

On each trip he lectured, always in his native German language, to groups of students and adults, even to a gathering of attorneys in the court in which his father had been forbidden to practice. The more he spoke, the healthier and stronger he became emotionally, mentally and physically.

He was rejuvenated as he discovered the new Germany, meeting new friends and developing a good support system of people who helped him find the truth about his father's death. He renewed an old friendship with his childhood companion, now Dr. Wolfgang Kreft, who had also become a well-known notar and a lawyer.

At their reunion, Wolfgang related an incident that had happened just before Ralph and his mother had left Germany. The two boys passed each other on the street, "and knowing that you were leaving, I wanted to wave to you, to say goodbye, but I knew it was too dangerous."

So, on Ralph's first trip back to Germany, the two reunited friends stood on the same spot where they had passed each other by in 1939 and shook hands. Wolfgang later told Ralph that the war didn't end for him until that day fifty-seven years later.

Gradually, the story of his father's death emerged. In the fall of 1938, the mayor, who was also police chief and a Nazi leader, wanted to demolish the synagogue and use the land to build a Gestapo headquarters.

Ralph's father strongly opposed the wishes of the mayor and the destruction of the synagogue. That opposition proved deadly. The coroner reported that Dr. Jacobson had committed suicide by hanging, when in reality he was followed to the garden and strangled by Nazi operatives.

In the late 1990s Dr. Wolfgang Kreft and his son, Thomas, prepared a ten page legal brief, citing the facts, which was presented to the city authorities.

Obviously the original death certificate, which bore the notation of 'suicide', had been fabricated by the coroner and by those in power. Through the efforts of Drs. Wolfgang and Thomas Kreft a new official death certification was issued and signed by the mayor on July 20, 1999. This certificate simply stated the date and place of Ernst Jacobson's birth and the date and place of his death – with no mention of the cause, thus righting the wrong that had been a part of the town's written history.

The St. Stephan windows played a momentous role in reconciling Ralph to the blatant anti-Semitism of his youth and to the circumstances of the death of his father. That reconciliation is continuously confirmed as he now lectures about the Holocaust regularly to school and adult groups in our community and in the United States.

The understanding and the resolution that was such a positive factor in Ralph's life was repeated many times over through the lives of others who have viewed the St. Stephan windows. Most particularly I have found a deep outpouring of honest affection and true respect for Chagall on the part of the German people.

In 1996, I read an article in an arts magazine announcing a trip to Vitebsk, Belarus, in July of the following year. The purpose of the trip was to celebrate the 110th birthday of Chagall, and to observe the re-opening of his parental home. The simple building, almost completely destroyed during World War II, was being restored after many years of neglect, through the efforts of a group of fifty-five Germans led by Dr. Christopher Goldmann, a theologian and art historian. The trip to Vitebsk was planned by Dr. Goldman, and after an exchange of correspondence, I joined the group of German citizens on this journey – the only American.

Dr. Goldmann had gathered a group of people known as the German Patrons of the Chagall House in Vitebsk and was in the process of raising the funds to pay for the restoration of Chagall's "modest wooden house." To call the group's members "Chagall fanatics" is simply an understatement. Doctors, business people, ministers, lawyers, teachers from all different parts of Germany had come together to help continue to raise the funds needed and to meet the government people in charge of the restoration.

The group was so knowledgeable about Chagall, his artwork, his friends and associates in the art world, that I felt I was in the presence of true

Chagallian scholars. As an example, on the bus trips we took to the areas surrounding Vitebsk, each one of them would either have a copy of *My Life*, Chagall's early autobiography, or *Burning Lights*, written by Chagall's first wife, Bella. They would read portions of the chapters aloud and have vigorous discussions – never mind what the passing scenery might be! Or they would have energetic symposiums at breakfast time.

All of it was in German. My Yiddish, a language which is based on Hebrew and German, helped me out a lot, and by the time the trip was over, I was fairly fluent in the German language.

Among the activities we attended during the week-long celebration, were dinner parties, and the opening of the Chagall Museum of Vitebsk. There I gave a lecture on some of the lithographs on loan from the Musée Chagall in Nice, and attended a major Friday evening event with the Jewish community of Vitebsk.

Throughout the week, I was reminded that while World War II was fought here a little more than fifty years ago, in this place were Germans, Russians, Jews and Christians all coming together in a time of celebration for an artist whose own life reflected the spirit of reconciliation.

On the last night of the celebration, an outdoor concert was given by a symphony orchestra in front of the town hall with the audience seated on a hillside overlooking the musicians. At its conclusion, all the lights were extinguished.

Then suddenly out of the darkness, spotlights shone directly on the nine violinists dressed in Hasidic garb, one in each of the seven windows on the fourth floor of the town hall, with one on the roof, and one in the clock tower, playing a moving Vivaldi selection. Obviously, after a momentary hush, the reaction of the audience was tumultuous, capturing the memory of Chagall's famous painting, *The Green Violinist* portraying a fiddler on a roof.

The outpouring of respect and affection for Chagall by the German people is demonstrated in many ways from the restoration of his parent's home in Vitebsk, Belarus, to the German bookstores where you can find Chagall biographies and catalogues with reproductions of his art, and to exhibitions of his work constantly drawing huge crowds in German cities. All this is rooted in Chagall's ultimate message of reconciliation as reflected in the windows of St. Stephan in Mainz.

What a climax the conception and the completion of the windows were in Chagall's life! The artist was eighty-nine years old when he started on the first sketches for the windows. To have created such a monument for understanding among nations and religions in his twilight years was a testament to the depth of his longing for world peace.

Above all, the brilliance of the windows' colors represents optimism and hope. Marc Chagall found that hope and his positive attitude toward life from the world of the Bible. The windows are a permanent reminder of Chagall's Biblical message of love for all the people of the world.

Chapter 7
The Women in Chagall's Life
and Other Reminiscences

One of the lectures that I often give is titled "Chagall and the Women in his Life," which describes the women, his mother, his six sisters, his two wives, his companion, his daughter and his granddaughters, shaped his personality. In some cases, they had a significant influence on his work. Swiss art historian George Schmidt once referred to Chagall as "an undeserved present to our century." So, too, were the women in his life. They are also a gift to the world. In the eleven years that I experienced a close bond of friendship with Chagall, on many occasions I saw, encountered, and gained an understanding of the important a role played by the women in his life. He was constantly surrounded by women who supported each of his artistic ventures. Thus, due to their devotion, he was able to accomplish so much in his lifetime. Consequently, my memories of my time with Chagall are interwoven with reminiscences of how deeply he felt about the women whose paths crossed his.

Chagall not only loved women, he had an enormous amount of respect for them. A favorite 1935 poster in our house is of an acrobat. Actually it is a woman dressed as a trapeze artist, balancing her life as if in a circus and surrounded with images of her house, her synagogue and her butcher shop. The husband, in profile, blesses her with a little kiss on her cheek. This was how Chagall viewed women, as multitasking individuals, balancing work and the demands of home, family and religion.

One of the lessons in my lecture is that Chagall had an emotional need to hold the hand of a woman. When you look at some of his paintings, such as *Red Lovers in the Sky*, *Lovers in the Moonlight*, or *Lovers in Lilac*, the passion that Chagall felt for the subject of lovers is unmistakable. No doubt about it – having your hand held by Chagall was an extraordinary experience. I can clearly recall my heart rate jumping from 72 to 150 on more than one occasion.

One day in the spring 1979, I was visiting with Marc and Vava Chagall in their home in France, to discuss some of the projects that I was working on for the Musée Chagall. During that conversation, Vava asked me if I would go to Israel with them in about six weeks.

Vava explained that Chagall had designed a gold coin based on the writings of the Prophet Isaiah. They were invited to attend the dedication of the coin at the Knesset with Prime Minister Menachem Begin speaking in honor of the occasion. The profits from the sales of reproductions of the coin would go to the building of apartments for young couples in Jerusalem.

I thought perhaps Vava wanted me to accompany them to do some translation from the Hebrew, or drive a car, or oversee the schedule for their two-week visit. However, when I asked her why she wanted me to go with them, she simply replied, "I need someone to hold Marc's hand."

Elaborating further, she said that unless Chagall was holding the hand of a woman, he could not function, and that she was getting too old, besides having too many duties associated with the visit, to be able to hold his hand all the time. Immediately I understood why she wanted me to travel with them to Israel.

Vava knew that I would have to talk to Ralph, and I would call her with an answer once I had returned home. When Ralph and I talked about the trip, he agreed I could meet them in Nice and fly with them to Israel. However, he said he had only one question for Vava. "If Chagall is holding Vivian's right hand, who will be holding her left hand?" A joke, but a meaningful indication of how Ralph always was looking after me.

I called Vava with the good news that I would accompany them, and relayed Ralph's question to her, to which she laughingly responded, "That, Vivian, is your problem, not mine!"

As it turned out, Marc and Vava decided that the trip would be too arduous for him to take at the time, and they sent me as their representative. It was a glorious event. At the reception following the Knesset presentation, the beautiful floral arrangement on the center table could have been copied directly from one of Chagall's magnificent paintings, and his spiritual presence was clearly a part of the entire dedication.

As Prime Minister Menachem Begin introduced me to Chagall's Israeli friends, I thought about Chagall and Vava. If in fact they had come to Jerusalem, I would be meeting all of these people, with Chagall holding my right hand while Vava would be graciously meeting other guests and dignitaries.

Five years before that trip to Israel, I had studied Chagall's family history to become familiar with the first woman who had a profound influence on his life – his mother, Feiga-Ita. Married at fifteen years of age, a year later, she had given birth to Marc, the first of nine children. Marc then had six sisters, Anita, Zena, Lisa, Manya, Rosa and Maraska, and only one brother, David. Another child had died in infancy.

Fiega-Ita was a model for modern day feminists. At a time when a woman's place was definitely in the home, she had her own little real estate business – arranging for and renting out small housing units on the family's property, and running a small grocery store.

As a young mother, she quickly realized that her eldest son, Marc, had to have the best education possible. She wanted him to attend classes other than Hebrew school, so she paid dearly the head of the Russian-speaking high school to admit her son. Clearly, this was the defining moment in his life for it was totally unheard for a Jewish woman to make such a request during the time of virulent anti-Semitism.

Feiga-Ita did not understand Marc's interest in drawing which became evident as he grew older. The Biblical teachings of the second commandment allow for no graven images. But she was more sympathetic to his talent than his father, taking him to see Yehuda Pen, a well-known Jewish artist with whom Marc ultimately studied. Once again, she had pushed Chagall to follow his dreams.

Chagall's love and affection for his mother was a guiding principle of his early life. At the age of thirty-five, in his 1922 autobiography, he describes Fiega-Ita as a powerful woman, although "She was tiny. In her heart she held a love for her children and for her book of prayers."

Bella, Chagall's first wife, was his soul mate and his muse. He sought her approval of all of his work, and she posed as a model for many of his early paintings. She was the daughter of a well-to-do jeweler, and was educated in music and literature, as well as in art.

Bella was eight years younger than Chagall. After a four-year courtship, the couple were married on July 25, 1915, and lived first in St. Petersburg, while Bella continued to study and write. She encouraged Chagall to illustrate books and create set and costume design for the Jewish theater in Moscow. For a time after the birth of their daughter, Ida, they returned to Vitebsk where he continued to paint. He also held the position of Commissar of Arts in the region.

The young family emigrated to Paris in 1922 which began a prolific period for Chagall. During this time he became a French citizen. He painted continuously, illustrating books and having numerous exhibitions of his work.

As the war clouds gathered over Europe, and the Nazis invaded France, their daughter, Ida, now a grown woman, convinced Chagall and Bella to flee first to the south of France. Then, with the help of two Americans, Hiram Bingham IV, a United States diplomat in Marseille and Varian Fry of the New York Emergency Rescue Committee, who worked tirelessly on behalf of writers, artists and other intellectuals in danger of persecution by the Nazis, the Chagalls escaped to the United States in May 1941.

For the next three years Chagall, while living in New York with Bella at his side, continued his painting. In the meantime, Ida became responsible for securing and secreting five hundred paintings plus hundreds of drawings of Chagall's from the Nazis during World War II. The Germans planned to confiscated the huge caché of artwork, but Ida managed to send the artwork from France to Spain and then to Portugal and finally to the United States.

In September 1944, tragedy struck when Bella fell ill with a strep throat, and after a short illness, died suddenly. Chagall was devastated by her loss because theirs had been a close, warm and passionate love. For the next nine months he sank into a dark depression, not once picking up a paint brush.

In Spring 1945, Ida, concerned about her father's well-being, introduced Chagall to Virginia Haggard. She was the daughter of a British diplomat. She had studied art and spoke fluent French. Virginia was married to John McNeil, a Scottish painter and theatrical designer. Trying to provide for her unsuccessful husband and little daughter, Jean, she assumed the role of Chagall's housekeeper. As the relationship intensified, they became friends, companions and lovers, and had a son together, David. However, the time Chagall and Virginia spent together was satisfying for each of them. They needed each other physically and intellectually.

Chagall had started painting again. During this time he created the set and costume design for George Balanchine's ballet, *The Firebird*. Recapturing the luminous quality and vivid colorations of his paintings for which he had become known, his artwork of the period also included illustrations for four tales from *The Arabian Nights*, that are viewed by critics as some of his finest lithographs.

Because of the differences in their religious backgrounds, Chagall would not marry her, and after seven years she left. Virginia eventually divorced McNeil and married a Belgian photographer, Charles Leirins.

Meanwhile, a most efficient Ida Chagall had taken charge of promoting her father's talent, setting up exhibitions, overseeing gallery sales, catalogues and commissions in New York and Paris. And after Chagall returned to France from the United States, in 1948, he had her bring back the artworks which were removed from France during World War II.

Ida's first marriage was to Michel Rapaport in 1934. In 1952, Ida's second marriage was to Franz Meyer, an art intellectual and art historian. They had a son, Piet, and twin daughters, Bella and Meret. Later, Franz Meyer was the Director of the Kunstmuseum in Basle, Switzerland, and, collaborating with Ida, wrote the definitive work on Chagall. The first edition was in 1961, published in German at DuMont Schauberg, Köln. A massive volume, it is the major source for information for Chagall scholars. It was translated into French and English in the early 1960s.

Franz Meyer writes of that collaborative work: "Ida Meyer-Chagall, the artist's daughter, handled the extensive photographic matter. During years of incessant work she collected all that was required for putting the book together and compiled the Classified Catalogue of reproductions, which number nearly fourteen hundred. That technical assistance was only a small part of what she did, for she opened the door to Chagall's world in the truest sense."

During my association with Chagall, I had gotten to know Ida well and appreciated her practical and brilliant mind. Her spirit was always warm and generous. She once thanked me for helping her father live longer, crediting my enthusiastic involvement with such projects as the harpsichord at the Musée Chagall as the motivation for Chagall's continued creation of his wonderful works of art.

After Virginia Haggard's bittersweet departure and Chagall's return to Paris, Ida once again came to the rescue. In 1952 she introduced Chagall to Valentina Brodsky, better known as Vava. She came from a Russian-Jewish background, and her family origins were aristocratic.

Chagall said with deep emotion, "When my father was hauling herrings, the Brodskys of Kiev were buying Tintorettos." Vava's family suffered financial ruin in the Russian Revolution, so as a young woman, she lived in Paris and in England, where she had a successful business career. She was twenty-five years younger than Chagall, but agreed to return to France to become Chagall's housekeeper, and eventually became his wife of thirty-three years.

Vava soon assumed and maintained control over all the elements of her husband's professional and artistic life. She was his Chief Executive Officer, managing director, secretary, treasurer and artistic agent, and encouraged him to widen his artistic horizons, applying his talent into ever more impressive projects, such as mosaics, stained glass windows, and tapestries.

Acting as his intermediary, Vava was the liaison between Chagall and the other artisans that worked with him to produce the astonishing range of his work. For his lithographs, it was Charles Sorlier; for the magnificent stained glass windows, it was Charles Marq; for the superb tapestries, it was Yvette Cauquil-Prince; and for the mosaics, it was Lino Milano; and Michel Tharin. These accounted for only a few talented artisians who worked with the master.

A sampling of the monumental works that Chagall created during the thirty-three years of their marriage includes the stained glass windows at the Cathedral at Reims, at the Metz Cathedral and at Hadassah Hospital in Jerusalem. Also the ceiling of the Paris Opera House, the *Peace* window at the United Nations, New York's Lincoln Center murals for the Metropolitan Opera, windows for the Chapelle des Cordeliers, in Sarrebourg, Moselle, France and tapestries hung in prominent locations around the world.

However, the relationship of Marc and Vava was not all business. Chagall expressed his deepening love for her poetically.

> ...With you I am young,
> My years fall like leaves,
> Somebody colors my paintings
> Which shine close to you...

And he said of her "My worries disappear one by one when Vava is near me." A mutual tenderness and devotion and an intimate affection for one another was very evident as you observed the two of them together. These feelings also permeated the many letters Vava wrote me over the years.

Bella Meyer and Meret Meyer, the artist's two granddaughters are as intelligent and beautiful as their mother, Ida. I have had the privilege of working with them on various projects on behalf of their grandfather.

These extraordinary women continue to convey the message of Marc Chagall's legacy to the world. The world has benefited greatly from their efforts. Bella, who lives in New York, has a doctorate in medieval art from the Sorbonne, and lectures on Chagall. In the February 2000 issue of *ARTnews*, Bella, remembers her grandfather as "very nice, funny and mischievous. Paintings were more to him than art, they were a sort of celebration of a mission, which was to find meaning and one's inner path. He was always asking us what we were looking for in life. I think I share his rather naïve hopes for peace, and if I inherit anything from him, it would be his pure heart."

Meret studied German literature and linguistics, philosophy and theater science and received a master's degree from the University of Cologne in all these subjects. She is very involved in the management of exhibitions, the archives, and the Comité Chagall, which is the entity qualified to authenticate works of art by Chagall. She organized a most successful exhibition of Chagall's works for an opening in December 2007. The exhibition, in the unlikely location of a large theme park in southwest Germany called Europa-Park, was seen by a record 100,000 people within five weeks.

Both of the granddaughters own artworks, documents, notebooks, photographs and other materials related to Chagall's creations, and serve on the Comité Chagall. The mission of this small, intimate organization, located in what was Ida Chagall's home in Paris, is to perpetuate and to safeguard the heritage of the great 20th century artist.

One of Ida's long kept promises regarding some of her father's artwork stirred up an international incident in 1990. Five suitcases containing one hundred and three of Chagall's drawings, sketches and a few paintings were picked up at Ida's home in Paris and transported to Israel by Jerusalem's mayor, Teddy Kollek, without any notice given to or authorization received from the French government.

According to Kollek, Ida had promised as far back as 1969 to donate the art work to the Israel Museum. He reported simply that he had received a phone call to go to Paris and take possession of the donation at the home of Ida, who was ill.

When I heard about the art work reaching Israel, I contacted the curator of the museum and made immediate arrangements to fly to Israel. I couldn't have been more excited as Stephanie Ruhama, the curator, assured me that I would be able to privately view the works in the museum's library. I would literally have Chagall all to myself!

I scarcely noticed a gentleman seated at the other end of the room study-ing some very interesting artwork. Stephanie introduced me to Joachim Pissarro, the great grandson of Camille Pissarro and mentioned my con-nection with Chagall. I told him that I admired his great grandfather's art and that I was honored to meet him. Joachim was preparing for a Pissarro exhibition at the museum, and he had work to do. I retreated to my end of the table to view what I had come for, the gift of Ida Chagall.

The drawings in India ink were spread out, and the entire subject matter of Chagall's love and memories of his birthplace came to life. His parents, the garden, the animals in the backyard, the house he lived in, and the people of Vitebsk were all present in this room. The drawings were superb, very delicate and simple and very elegant. No wonder the French govern-ment was so distressed!

There is an amusing footnote to this account of my meeting Joachim Pis-sarro. I had planned to spend part of one more day at the library, making notes, but then Stephanie called me at my hotel that evening and asked if I could come in a little early the next day.

She had told Pissarro that I was a swimming teacher. He said he had a problem with his goggles fitting properly. Could I help him? We agreed to meet in Stephanie's office the next morning. Of course I would be glad to be of assistance to the great grandson of one of my favorite artists.

The next morning in a small powder room near Stephanie's office, equipped with my own goggles which I had placed in my briefcase, I showed Joachim how to wet them and how to place them correctly over the eyes with one hand and the other holding the strap that goes around the head. Aha! A moment of silence and surprise on his part.

It's no wonder that he had trouble with water leaking into the goggles. Obviously, he had not put them on properly all these years. A huge smile and a warm thank you followed, and then each of us went back to work in the library, new found friends in the worlds of lap swimming and art!

Ralph lightheartedly reminds me from time to time how focused I can become when working on any project having to do with Chagall. In 1992 I had decided to develop a lecture about the Chagall windows at the St. Stephan Church in Mainz.

Our breakfast room table was groaning under the weight of a stack of books on the subject including my two Bibles, a slide projector, and carousel with a collection of slides showing the individual windows. To prepare a lecture on a new subject can take weeks and sometimes even months of my time. Much research must be done in viewing Chagall's works and conveying his messages to portray in the most accurate way possible to my audience.

Sometimes the dishes are left in the sink, beds are unmade, phone calls are not returned, and other duties not performed, as I concentrate entirely on the lecture preparation. Such was the case one day when Ralph asked me to repair the closure clip on his golf pants. "Just hang the pants in the closet and I will take care of it later this afternoon," I replied.

Of course I did not repair the clip that afternoon, and two days later he approached me with the same request. I replied with the same answer. Five days later, Ralph once again approached me with the pants in one hand and the clip in the other. He stood directly in front of me at my work table. "Chagall would like to play golf tomorrow on Pinehurst Course #2 at 11:32 a.m. Do you think you can get the pants ready for him?" Needless to say, the message was loud and clear. "Chagall's" golf pants were ready in less than an hour.

And there is just one more hand-holding memory which has become one of my favorite stories. It occurred when Ralph and I traveled to France for Chagall's 95th birthday in July 1982. We had a meeting with him on the morning of the celebration, and as the conversation was taking place, Chagall took my left hand and grasped it on the top with his right hand.

With that, as he was speaking, he made slow circular motions with his thumb on my hand several times. Looking directly at Ralph, he spoke in French, saying "Elle a beaucoup d'enthousiame." Ralph, of course, agreed. However, when I turned to Ralph and whispered in English that I was being turned on by a 95 year old man, my husband of twenty-five years looked at me with a huge smile on his face in reply. He understood.

Later that afternoon while I was finishing dressing for the party, Ralph came to me, and without speaking a word, quietly took his right hand and reached for my left hand. Then he made the exact same circular motions with his thumb that Chagall had done that morning. I waited a few seconds, watching him emulate Chagall's hand holding move. Looking at Ralph, I sadly told him that nothing was happening. I commented, "Maybe when you are 95, but not at 54!"

Chapter 8
The Undiscovered Chagall

Where does one go to find a piece of Chagall's artwork? Of course, his paintings are exhibited in major museums and galleries in Europe, Israel, the United States, Asia and Australia, and his creative genius in the media of stained glass windows, mosaics and large-scale murals in prominent places continues to receive considerable public attention.

However many hidden, rarely viewed works of the artist may also bring delight to the viewer. As I became acquainted with Chagall and the enormous output of his artistic talent, it became a challenge for me to seek out and find these works of the "undiscovered Chagall."

For instance, in such small, out of the way European museums as the Von der Heydt Museum in Wuppertal, Germany, or in the Museum of Contemporary Art on Greece's Andros Island, examples of Chagall's work are on display. In the United States, two Chagall prints are at the Montana Museum of Art & Culture in Missoula. Other works are at the Lawrence University of Appleton, Wisconsin, as well as at the Dixon Gallery and Gardens in Memphis, Tennessee.

The undiscovered Chagall works are rarely ever mentioned by lecturers on Chagall, or in the many books written about him and his work. You may acquire a clue from travel books such as Fodor's or Frommer's, but more often than not, a traveler will unknowingly come across a church with stained glass windows or a lovely mosaic done by Chagall. Such is the case of *The Story of Baby Moses*. This inspired mosaic is located above the baptistery of the Cathedral in Vence, France.

Why aren't the lesser known works of Chagall recorded in a more thorough and incisive way? Is it because of the sheer number? Or is it because art critics and writers simply don't know about them? Or it is because the art world doesn't attach enough importance to anything but the best recognized paintings and other works of Chagall?

As a lecturer, I am extremely frustrated by this situation. Often after giving a talk, a member of the audience will approach me and tell me of an undiscovered Chagall work that he has stumbled across in a most unlikely place. A good example of this is the woman who mentioned seeing glowing stained glass windows by Chagall at the Union Church in Pocantico Hills, New York, or the person who referred to a set of beautiful stained glass windows in the small All Saints Church at Tudeley in Kent, England. What pleasure I had to visit both churches and to view the wonderful windows.

I have also visited seldom seen pieces of Chagall's creative output such as the mosaic of *The Message of the Odysseus*, at the Law School Library at the University of Nice in France; the stained glass windows at the Chichester Cathedral in Sussex, England; and a tapestry of the *Prophet Jeremiah* at the Helfaer Jewish Community Center In Milwaukee, Wisconsin.

I have found Chagall in unexpected places. Once, after a lecture, a woman in the audience took me out to her car to show me a Chagall artwork, nestled in the trunk of a green Volvo. The work was a framed lithograph, a scene of Paris, the Eiffel Tower, lovers and angels in a bright yellow background with washes of purple, orange and a paler yellow.

Originally done to announce an art exhibition in Paris, a lithograph was also created without any printing. Chagall had signed it twice, once on the lithograph and once on the matting. This beautiful work was purchased by the woman's grandfather, a doctor, who gave it to his son, who then in turn handed it down to his daughter, the present owner.

The experience of having people proudly show me a treasured Chagall work is always one of the joys of learning to know the man and his work. On a trip to Israel, visiting friends in a kibbutz, I was asked if I wanted to see an original Chagall which belonged to a couple living in a nearby apartment.

As I entered their very small apartment, I was led into the bedroom, where a large drawing of Vitebsk done in the 1920's was displayed. It was given to them by the woman's Russian father, Leo Koenig, an artist, art critic, and an émigré living in Paris in 1929, who was befriended by Chagall. The drawing had been signed by Chagall and he had added a lovely inscription in Yiddish. How extraordinary, I thought, even in a tiny apartment in a desert kibbutz one can find a Chagall!

Another surprise took place in Tel Aviv, when I was visiting in the home of Joseph Boxenbaum, one of Chagall's closest friends. In the dining room stood a room divider, a French "paravent," in four sections. Each section was a work of Chagall's art: the first, a gorgeous light-filled backdrop with themes of Paris and the Eiffel Tower; a second panel of St. Paul de Vence with the ever-floating lovers; a third with a bright summer sun shining on a bird; and the fourth panel a vase of colorful flowers.

The four paneled divider looked very much like the one in Ida's home in Paris. This screen is reproduced in the book *Chagall: The Lithographs* by Charles Sorlier, Chagall's lithographer. Perhaps only three or four similar artworks in the world, and I was fortunate to see two of them.

Possibly my most unusual "find" of Chagall's work was in the powder room of the home of a prominent woman in Chicago's art community. I was invited to have tea and cakes with a group of art patrons. As I was leaving, I took a few minutes to quietly ask the hostess about the unique Chagall hanging in her powder room.

She told me that in 1958 when Chagall came to present a lecture at the University of Chicago, she and some friends had invited Chagall and Vava to lunch at Jacques Restaurant on Michigan Avenue. After ordering lunch, Chagall was getting fidgety. He needed to be doing something, so he moved the set luncheon plate and silverware, and spread out a large white linen napkin. He then asked his hostess and the other women guests to look in their purses and find their lipsticks which he commandeered.

Three were selected by Chagall, and with those he drew a brilliant tree in shades of red, rose and pale pink. By the time the waiters had served lunch, this exquisite drawing was completed and presented to the hostess as a gift. She had it framed and hung it in her powder room. I didn't have the heart to ask her why she had hidden this personal treasure in such an inconspicuous place, but I was honored to have had this delightful visual experience.

Another side to this great artist was Chagall's literary capabilities. The American novelist, Henry Miller, once said of Chagall: "He is a poet with wings of a painter." And indeed he preferred the company of poets and writers to that of his fellow painters. He was an acknowledged poet in his own right.

Chagall wrote poems in Yiddish, Russian and French. In 1975, in Geneva, Gérald Cramer published forty-one of Chagall's poems from the years 1909 to 1972, and the volume was illustrated with twenty-one woodcuts by the artist.

Chagall's poetry flows smoothly, it does not rhyme. Like his paintings his poetry has an element of mysticism and a magical realism. Someone once asked him, "How come you paint the same things over and over?" to which he replied, "the Russian alphabet has but 22 letters that a poet uses over and over again."

Explaining Chagall's statement, distinguished scholar and author Benjamin Harshav notes that Chagall's culture was really Yiddish, but he often masked it as Russian. The Hebrew and Yiddish languages have 22 letters, rather than the actual 32 letters in the Russian alphabet.

The literary Chagall is an important part of the undiscovered Chagall. Naturally, many published quotations from Chagall, spring from interviews and from conversations with his close friends and members of his artistic circle:

- "Great art picks up where nature ends."
- "I am out to introduce a psychic shock into my painting, one that is always motivated by pictorial reasoning: that is to say, a fourth dimension."
- "In our life there is a single color, as on an artist's palette, which provides the meaning of life and art. It is the color of love."

But Chagall was much more than a sum of his quotations and his poetry. He also gave beautifully written speeches at special events, when his art work was unveiled or honored – speeches that dealt with the conditions of the world and the relationship between art and humanity. Many of them can be found in an unusual book, *Chagall, a Retrospective*, published in 1995.

Written and edited by Jacob Baal-Teshuva, an art critic, independent curator and a friend of Chagall. This handsome and comprehensive study, presents skillfully excerpted pieces from critical sources, as well as interviews with Chagall, and letters, essays, poetry and lectures by the artist himself.

The speeches include an early one Chagall gave at Mt. Holyoke College during the years of World War II, and remarks he made on accepting the Erasmus Prize in 1960. The prize is given by a Dutch non-profit organization to individuals or institutions that have made notable contributions to European culture, society or social science. Remarks that Chagall made at the unveiling of the Paris Opera House ceiling and the murals at the

Metropolitan Opera House, as well as those he gave at the dedication of the *Peace* window at the United Nations, are also included.

In 1922 Chagall published his memoirs which were written in Yiddish, then translated into Russian and later into French by Bella. *My Life* was written in Moscow when Chagall was thirty-five years old. The text is accompanied by twenty plates that Chagall prepared to illustrate his life story. Reprinted in many languages, it remains one of the most inventive of all autobiographies, particularly as it describes his early family life in Vitebsk, and his mother and father.

This valuable facet of Chagall's life, the literary Chagall, gives a greater depth to understanding his personality. And like the undiscovered Chagall, it is one that I enthusiastically share with my readers.

"Some have reproached me for incorporating poetry into my paintings, but show me a single masterpiece that does not have some poetry in it."

Marc Chagall

Chapter 9
Angel Stories

As I look back over the years of my association with Chagall from our initial meeting to the present day, I have had the good fortune to meet many individuals that I call my Chagall Angels. These wonderful strangers, some of whom have become good friends, have gone above and beyond the call of their regular routines to assist me as I traveled on behalf of Chagall. Or they have provided me with needed support when I have been faced with a problem that didn't seem readily solvable.

These people are miraculously connected to Chagall without meeting him or having a conversation with him. These stories are so important to me because they show that connection of respect, admiration and love which Chagall believed made all things possible. This is the reason that these people went out of their way with their friendship and assistance, and continue to do so.

The story of Chagall's sweater is a good illustration of finding a Chagall angel. During my presidency of the American Friends of the Chagall Biblical Museum, I was preparing for a trip to France. I stopped at Marshall Fields on Michigan Avenue to pick up Chagall's favorite Frango Chocolate Mints. This time, however, I wanted to bring some extra gifts for him and Vava.

As I browsed, I selected a soft wool scarf in hues of yellow, orange and red for Vava, and then my eye caught a counter laden with beautiful men's sweaters. This would be a perfect gift for Chagall, who always dressed in a casual manner. I chose a brown tweed with specks of color running through it.

But what size would be the right one, medium or large?

I enlisted the help of a saleswoman. I mentioned it was a gift for an older gentleman, and she asked me "Is he in a nursing home?" I couldn't help myself, but I dissolved into laughter, as I had a momentary vision of Chagall strutting along the aisles of Marshall Fields.

After I caught my breath, I explained that the sweater was for a very lively gentleman who happened to be my friend, Marc Chagall, the noted artist. She immediately said, "Then we definitely must decide on the correct size. Do you see any customers in the immediate vicinity who are about his height and weight?"

I noticed a young man who was about the size of Chagall. The sales-woman approached him and asked him if he would willing try on two sweaters for a customer. He kindly agreed. With his assistance we determined that the medium was the proper size. The saleswoman thanked him for his help and said, "This sweater is a gift for the artist, Marc Chagall."

I thought the young man was going into cardiac arrest; he had such a stunned look on his face. "Marc Chagall!" he gasped. Then he quickly recovered. "I am a student at the Art Institute of Chicago. What an honor to have been of service to you and to such a great artist."

My gifts for Chagall and Vava were warmly received, and some months later Chagall was photographed for the front cover of the Paris magazine, *Le Figaro*, wearing his brown tweed sweater. Proudly, I took a copy of the magazine to the Art Institute to show the young man. Unfortunately, I had not gotten his name, and with just a general description of him, the secretary at the school was unable to identify him. For me, he was an unsung Chagall angel.

Another event took place when I was returning from Israel after representing Chagall at the dedication of the Prophet Isaiah gold coin. I had planned to take a Wednesday evening flight to Nice in order to meet with Vava and Chagall at a pre-arranged time at 11:30 on Thursday morning.

This was an important visit since it involved my giving them a full description of the dedication, the people who attended, and greetings from Prime Minister Begin and other friends of Chagall. Upon telephoning Air France to confirm my flight, I was informed that the pilots and flight attendants had canceled the evening flight to Nice, because of a planned strike. I was frantic. I explained my need to be in St. Paul de Vence at 11:30 Thursday morning to meet with Chagall, and Air France said they would try to help me. How? They didn't know.

An hour later, the supervisor for Air France Tel Aviv called to let me know that there would be a final pre-strike flight from Tel Aviv to Paris, leaving at 7 p.m. Wednesday night. I could stay overnight in Paris at an airport hotel and then very early the next morning, fly from Paris to Nice, arriving in time to take a taxi to St. Paul de Vence, reaching my destination by 11:30 a.m.

I agreed to the alternate arrangements and took the Tel Aviv – Paris flight. As I checked in, the Air France representative assured me that my bags would be "on board." I could not understand what she meant. After we were in flight for about four hours, I felt the plane descending.

Where were we? Was the plane in trouble? I began to say a prayer, and thought of my husband, Ralph, and our two sons, Ernest and Daniel. I was interrupted by the pilot's announcement that the plane was making an unscheduled, but necessary, stop in Nice. After a brief stop, he said, there will be an immediate departure for Paris.

As I was mulling over this surprising announcement, the flight attendant came and told me the landing was being made for me and a few other people, and that as soon as the plane landed to unbuckle my seatbelt and be ready to leave the plane immediately. My bags would be at the bottom of the stairs.

Deplaning, I saw a car on the tarmac, and it was for me! My bags were carried by a representative of Air France to the car, and with an au revoir, I was ushered into the vehicle. I was met at the terminal by another representative who helped me through customs, and then I was whisked out the door to a waiting taxi that took me to the Hotel Negresco, the finest hotel in Nice.

By the time I arrived at the hotel I was emotionally exhausted, but it finally dawned on me that Air France had made a special landing, not only for me, but for their national treasure, Marc Chagall. I think that they too understood the importance of the meeting and did not want him to be disappointed. Thank you, Air France. You are an airline of fantastic Chagall angels.

In more recent years, after Ralph and I moved to North Carolina, I organized a trip to Chicago for people in our community to view the outstanding art works that Chagall created for the city and paintings that hang in the galleries of the Art Institute of Chicago.

On the afternoon of our arrival, I went to the Art Institute to make sure that the paintings about which I would lecture on the following day were hung and not on loan to some other museum. *The Rabbi of Vitebsk, Naissance,* and *The Juggler* were all in their proper places, but where was my favorite painting, *White Crucifixion?*

I searched for the curator, who guaranteed me that the painting was in the building somewhere. But I was panicky. I had first seen this painting when I was nine years old and now I was prepared to give a lecture about it, and there was no painting.

I returned to my hotel in a state of depression. I had arranged a month in advance for these paintings to be available as the subjects of my lecture.

Late in the day, I received a call from the curator, telling me that the *White Crucifixion* had been located. "I called our staff that moves our paintings. That particular painting had been taken to the vault by mistake. By 9:00 tomorrow morning, it will be hanging in the 20th century gallery, along with the other Chagall works."

I thanked her profusely. I suspect that a Chagall angel was at work. Because the painting was a Chagall, she must have put extra energy into locating his most important work at the museum.

And speaking of lectures, I have even found Chagall angels in shoe stores. What is the connection between lectures on Chagall and a shoe store? There are tennis shoes, jogging shoes, and basketball shoes, but what about lecture shoes? For a long time I couldn't find a decent pair of shoes to wear while giving one of my lectures. Teachers, and some sales-people, must have the same problem.

Standing in a confined area for a certain length of time requires well-built footwear, which so far had eluded me. A friend recommended a particular line of women's shoes. I accessed the line's website on the Internet and called the nearest retailer.

I was told that the shoe that would fit my requirements was a black suede tie-up oxford with a very good arch support. I arranged to have a pair in my size set aside for me, and several days later when I went to the store, there was a box at the check-out counter, neatly labeled "Lecture shoes for Jacobson."

The shoes were a perfect fit and absolutely comfortable. The manager asked about the subject of my lectures. I told him, the artist, Marc Chagall. Perhaps he was an admirer of Chagall but this was another Chagall an-gel experience. I could now lecture without discomfort, and the manager even gave me a special 50% discount on my purchase.

And there are Chagall angels in the Tennessee warehouse distribution center of a book publisher. Taschen, the well-known German publisher of books on art and architecture some years ago had published a wonderful paperback on Chagall by Ingo F. Walther and Rainer Metzger. I had used the book as reference material in my lectures, and had also kept some copies on hand for my lecture audiences and friends.

At one point when I contacted the Los Angeles office of Taschen to place a re-order for one hundred of the books, I was told that they were no lon-ger going to publish the book. Instead, the decision was made to go to another format – a portfolio of ten reproductions of Chagall's artwork with a very short explanation of each one. I was terribly disappointed.

I called the Taschen client distribution warehouse in Jackson, Tennessee, from which I had ordered books in quantity previously, only to be told that indeed the book was no longer available. After a few days, I again called the distribution center to make absolutely sure that they did not have this book on their shelves

Suddenly, a Chagall angel appeared on the warehouse computer screen. Amazingly 2,500 of the Walther/Metzger books were available for purchase! No one at Taschen seemed to have any information about who ordered the books, or how they were received.

No matter. In my mind, I am doing cartwheels and twirling a baton on the front lawn. I love this moment. Tinti Dey of Taschen took my order. I could see her shaking her head while I am giving her my credit card number. Then I told her about Chagall angels. "They have been a part of my life since September 1974 when I first met the master."

An astonished Tinti tells me that this calls for a drink. Across 3000 miles, I decided to join her. I opened up the refrigerator and took out a bottle of peach wine. I poured a glass and gave a big l'chaim to my friend Chagall.

An individual who became so much more than a Chagall angel was my friend and my teacher in the technical aspects of illustrating my lectures. Chuck Olin was known as one of Chicago's best and brightest documentary makers.

As a matter of fact, Olin's *Palette of Glass: The America Windows of Marc Chagall* about the making of the Chagall's stained glass windows for the Art Institute of Chicago, won him an Emmy.

Olin completed another documentary about Chagall's work, titled *The Gift*, which traced Chagall's entire process creating the monumental *Four Seasons* mosaic in Chicago. These films that were made in 1974 and 1978, respectively, were my introduction to Chuck Olin and his work.

I realized early on that having some visual enhancement for my lectures was necessary, so I turned to Chuck Olin. In true Chagallian angel fashion, he brought me into his studio and led me through the intricacies of slides, projectors, carousels, advising me not only on the tricks for smooth operation, but what type of equipment to buy. It was one thing to order a set of slides from a museum or some other source, but it was quite another to learn how to use slides effectively in giving my lectures. For that I will always be grateful to Chuck Olin.

This master filmmaker also shared with me many slides for my lectures about *The Four Seasons* and the *America Windows*. I was particularly fascinated by the image of the Chagall paintbrushes. In this charming photo taken by Chuck, and later made into a slide, the foreground focuses on a group of brushes with oranges, reds, yellows and whites on the tips of the brushes contrasted by the brown wooden stems, while in the background are the *America Windows*. I have used the slide regularly at the conclusion of my lectures, while reading the lines of Chagall's *The Color of Love*.

Some years ago I gave a lecture at Fearrington Village outside Pittsboro, North Carolina, and as was my custom, I used the slide. About six months later while preparing for a lecture in Raleigh, I couldn't find the slide. I went through my entire slide collection, books, and materials for lectures and finally gave up and called Chuck. Although he didn't have the negative, he informed me that since I had a photo which had been made from the slide, I could now have a slide made from the photo. It wouldn't be as sharp as the original, but it would be close enough.

About a year later I gave another lecture at Fearrington Village. When I had finished, the audio-visual person who was putting away the screen and projector came up to me with an extra carousel in one hand, and the lost slide in the other. "Do these belong to you?" he queried.

He explained that in order to put the equipment back in the cabinet properly, he had to move some items. He pulled out the carousel with the missing slide neatly tucked into one of the holders.

I could not believe how happy I was to see the image again. It was as if Chagall were saying that when I go to an exhibition and see my drawings and paintings, it is like meeting an old friend again. That is what it was like for me. Chagall angels sometimes hide in small closets near Pittsboro, North Carolina, to watch over a precious possession.

Chuck Olin graciously accepted my invitation to come to Pinehurst and to give a program on his two documentary films about Chagall when our local synagogue was planning the "Chagall in Pinehurst" fundraising project some years ago. The documentaries were shown on a large screen, using a 16 mm projector. Chuck's accompanying lecture gave the audience a unique insight into the making of the film, and what it was like to work with the artist.

However, there was a major problem. The films were more than twenty-five years old, the colors had faded considerably and had taken on a light pink overcast. After the conclusion of Chuck's presentation we discussed the problem. He suggested since he had shipped all the copies of the film to me in the previous year, would I please review the copies to see if there were any that were worth transferring to DVD and video?

For this task, I turned to my friend, Ron Sutton, a retired professor of film at the American University in Washington, D.C. He agreed to help me with the project and one Saturday afternoon, arrived at my house with a 16 mm projector.

We settled down to start the process of grading the seven copies of the film. As the day wore on, we became more and more discouraged. I can remember my sadness, sitting with Ron, evaluating the films for clarity and color. We reviewed our grades for the first six and decided that the whole idea would appear to be a lost cause.

Ron loaded the seventh and final copy into the projector, and from nowhere, this incredible beautiful Chagall angel appeared. We were overwhelmed. The film projected on my living room wall had all the depth and breadth of what we were looking for in order to transfer the film to a DVD and a video. It received the highest grade possible. At first speechless, we uttered words, "This is unbelievable," while smiling and laughing.

The DVD and video transfer was funded by the Chagall Foundation and has become available to the public. These Olin creations are the very best of all the documentaries on Chagall.

Sadly, Chuck Olin passed away in January 2005. Digital imaging had changed dramatically from 1978 when I first met Chuck to the first few years of the 21st century. We had several discussions regarding changing the slide format for my lectures to a power point computer-generated presentation. Chuck's last words to me in October 2004 were that he didn't feel that a power point presentation would bring out the vibrancy of the Chagall colors that I had on the slides, and he recommended I stay with the slides, which I did.

About a month after Chuck passed away, I received an email from Maurice Mahler, a retired creative director and artist from Madison Avenue in New York City. He is a lecturer on several artists, including Picasso, Edward Hopper, and Chagall. He contacted me because I was listed on the Internet as a Chagall lecturer, and he wanted to find out how to handle some of the questions he was continuously asked at his lectures on Chagall.

Over time we became close long-distance friends, but more importantly, he was a Chagall angel that showed up at the right moment to take Chuck Olin's place. Maurice is just as kind and generous with his time and his expertise as Chuck had been.

For instance, Maurice realized that the Kodak projectors were becoming obsolete and through his contacts, he was able to secure a second projector from the University of Texas, should it be that I would ever need one. Now, however, my massive slide image library is all digitized and I present lectures via PowerPoint software. This allows for total integration of image, sound, and commentary.

Maurice has helped me immeasurably by having slides made and adjusted so I can continue using the slide format with my lectures. He is also a great researcher on Chagall, turning up little known facts, and bits of information that we share in our lectures. An example of this is his serious quest to locate the gravesite of Chagall's first wife, Bella.

Noting a caption on a photo of Bella's gravesite indicating that she was buried in New Jersey, Maurice set about finding the exact location. Learning no records existed for her in New Jersey, he widened his inquiries by calling the historical society in Cranberry Lake, New York, where the Chagalls had a country home during World War II when they lived in the United States.

Subsequently, his search led him to the Riverside Funeral Chapel in New York City. From the chapel, he retrieved the names of the cemeteries with which it was affiliated within New York State. He started calling individual cemeteries. The fourth cemetery he contacted was The Stephen Wise Free Synagogue Cemetery in Armonk, near White Plains, and he was rewarded by hearing the words, "We have Bella."

Maurice describes his feelings on a recent visit to the gravesite of Chagall's first love. "There is more than a simple footstone. It has an amazing headstone that is a piece of Chagall art – a beautiful heart with a hand holding a bouquet of flowers. Was it carved in marble by Chagall himself? I still look for the answer. As I placed a stone on the gravesite, I thought that there is so much love there."

Just as in Chagall's paintings a recurring figure of an angel appears, so it is that I have had an army of angels, like Maurice Mahler, and the other wonderful and helpful people described in this chapter, looking after me as I continue my mission to share Chagall's message.

Chapter 10
The Job Tapestry: The Beginning

Chagall's *Job* tapestry, which has hung in the lobby of the Rehabilitation Institute of Chicago for more than thirty years, was the last major work created by the man whose art has given hope and inspiration to generations. The saga of this unusual commission stretched over a period of four years, from its inception to the day the completed tapestry was unveiled and dedicated.

The story begins at a chance meeting on a beautiful sunlit morning in 1982 when Ralph and I were in France for the celebration of Chagall's 95th birthday. However, my account of the facts needs a preface.

In the early days while I was working with Chagall at his Biblical Message Museum, Pierre Provoyeur, the museum's director, had spoken about a work of Chagall's that was exhibited in Milwaukee at the Helfaer Jewish Community Center, less than one hundred miles from my Chicago home. The work, with which I was not familiar, was described by Provoyeur as a tapestry of the Prophet Jeremiah, woven by Yvette Cauquil-Prince of Paris, and whose design had been created by Chagall.

Upon my return to Chicago I immediately went to see this fourteen by nineteen foot magnificent work of art that has a profound and spiritual impact on the viewer. And just as quickly, I thought, why don't we have a Chagall tapestry in Chicago?

For a city with its world-renowned architecture and the outdoor sculptures by Picasso, Calder, Miro and DuBuffet, Chicago wasn't just, as the song goes, "my kind of town." It was a world-class city. Chicago already had the Chagall mosaic, *The Four Seasons*, and the stained glass panels of the *America Windows* at the Art Institute of Chicago. So why not a tapestry? Chicago would be the only city in the United States with three major works in these different media by the master, Marc Chagall.

The thought was idealistic, and I instinctively knew the limitations that Chagall would place on my idea for a tapestry for Chicago. It must have an Old Testament subject. It must be placed in a social service setting open to the public, and the design by Chagall would have to be executed by Yvette Cauquil-Prince.

I kept this fantastic dream inside of my head and heart until it spontaneously surged to reality on that morning in July 1982 in a small inn in St. Paul de Vence. Ralph and I had just met Dr. Henry Betts, Vice-Chairman and Medical Director of the Rehabilitation Institute of Chicago, because of a mutual friend, John Cartland, treasurer of the Institute and president of our city's Museum of Contemporary Art

As we joined the two men for breakfast at Le Hameau, Dr. Betts wondered what is the purpose of your trip. He had a summer place nearby, and was delighted to meet fellow Chicagoans. When Ralph told him about our plans to attend Chagall's birthday celebration, Dr. Betts said reflectively, "All my life, I have wanted a Chagall work of art for my patients."

That was it. Very simple. Very direct. Just as simply, and just as directly, I responded to his long time dream, with a promise borne of my own vision of a tapestry for Chicago. Very calmly, I said, "If you want a Chagall for your patients, I will acquire one for you."

I was struck that God had sent me the first of many Chagall angels for the tapestry project. There were scores of angels involved in the project who suddenly appeared at the most crucial times with a skill, or money, or a spiritual or personal connection, or an idea to help with our struggles to bring this artwork to Chicago.

And now, seated across from me was this doctor, a lifelong advocate for the disabled, who wanted to bring art to his patients. As Dr. Betts later wrote in the introductory brochure for the *Job* tapestry:

> *Art is many things to those who are disabled. At once,*
> *it is a celebration, a vehicle for expressing and, at*
> *times, enduring the tragic. It is also a language,*
> *universally understood, which asks nothing but the*
> *sensitivity and the humanity of the viewer.*

Here was a man who was thinking above and beyond himself, a man who wanted to elevate the spirits of the disabled and wanted to motivate them despite their disabilities to have a positive outlook on life. He wanted to give them hope, to give them beauty and to give them something created by the world's greatest living artist.

"What kind of art work were you thinking about?" I asked him. All the while I was thinking about the tapestry and praying inwardly that this would be his choice. It wasn't. He had been thinking about a stained glass window for the chapel on the mezzanine floor of the hospital.

I didn't panic, I didn't mention the tapestry or my dream, and I just listened as he continued on about the spiritual aspects of some of Chagall's work.

As he talked, I began to organize a committee in my mind that would have to operate outside of the Institute. This would be the group that would commission the artwork and give it to the hospital as a gift. I had a feeling of tremendous inner strength, because I was confident that I could change his mind from a stained glass window to a tapestry to be hung in the main lobby of the building.

We arranged to meet later that day at the lovely outdoor pool in Vence to discuss the matter and to formulate a strategy for presenting the idea to Chagall at a private meeting which had been scheduled later in the week.

Dr. Betts mentioned that he would like to bring his wife and six-year old daughter with him that afternoon, and on an impulse I suggested to him that perhaps his daughter would like a swimming lesson.

I had celebrated my 29th year as a swimming teacher and my 20th year as a swimming instructor-trainer for the American Red Cross. My experience had taught me that the offer of a free private one hour swimming lesson could work wonders in getting me anywhere, any place, any time. I was not above using such an offer as a persuasive tool to change Dr. Betts' thoughts about his suggested window.

As it turned out, six year old Amanda wanted a diving, rather than a swimming lesson. At the conclusion of the lesson, I had my doubts that I really had gained any credible advantage. However, when we returned to the group, and were enjoying the delightful park-like atmosphere, Dr. Betts turned to me and said, "Maybe a stained glass window in the chapel isn't such a good idea after all."

I held my breath. Was this the time to present the tapestry concept? I waited a few moments for his further explanation. "I've given my original idea some serious consideration, and believe it's not such a good one. First of all, there aren't that many people that use the chapel, and second, what kind of security and protection would be needed for a window?"

Of course, I agreed immediately, and then went on to say quietly, but firmly, "Perhaps the way to resolve the question is to have a tapestry based on a Biblical theme to be hung in the lobby. The lobby location would be an open space for patients and the public to appreciate the vibrant colors and the subject matter of a Chagall."

Dr. Betts was inspired with the idea of a tapestry. He was committed to the belief that art enhances the process of healing, as evidenced by the collection of posters, photos and other artistic expressions that he had had placed on the walls of the hospital to make life easier for the patients going through difficult and necessary rehabilitation.

Although I had heard many good things about the Rehabilitation Institute of Chicago, I had never visited it. Ironically, in the summer of 1977, I had the opportunity to teach aquatic rehabilitation in an Israeli hospital, and the doctors and therapists there had all spoken highly of the world-renowned reputation of the Institute and Dr. Betts.

When I related this to Dr. Betts, he naturally invited me for a special tour as soon as we returned home. He also pointed out that Vava had visited the Institute when the Chagalls were in Chicago in 1974 for the dedication of *The Four Seasons* mosaic. That visit had followed his introduction to both Marc and Vava briefly in 1965. What a plus this information would be when I met with Vava and Marc Chagall later in the week!

I must say at this point that I had not shared any of my secret thoughts about the tapestry with my husband Ralph who listened intently with his attorney's ear to the conversations I had been having with Dr. Betts. Although he had a lot of questions for me when we returned to our hotel, he knew that once I had an idea and it was something that I really wanted, it was, as the French say, *fait accompli*.

As always, I had his love and support. If there is one person in the world who knew where I was coming from and where I wanted to go, it was Ralph Jacobson. I believe that I needed only one person to believe in my dreams, and I am fortunate to have that person as my husband.

Two days later Ralph and I attended the 95th birthday of Chagall at his home, La Colline, set in the hills of Provence. It was the first time that Ralph had accompanied me to Chagall's home, so it was a memorable occasion. About twenty intimate friends, colleagues and family were there for this great celebration. When Chagall was passed a plate of chocolates, he started to take one, but Vava waved her finger to signal "no more," while giving him a fierce Russian stare. Looking straight back at her, in front of all the guests that had come to honor him, Chagall stuck out a little bit of his tongue at her, and with glaring eyes, reached out for two of the largest chocolate petit-fours. I laughed to myself. No one, including Vava, was going to tell him what or what not to eat on his 95th birthday.

I had been looking forward all week to our Saturday morning private meeting with Chagall two days later. As Ralph and I waited in the beautiful living room at La Colline, our eyes were drawn to all the glorious works of the artist, particularly the one over the fireplace of a bride and groom, with the Eiffel Tower in the background.

Vava soon appeared and explained that Chagall was in his atelier, so I went right to the point, telling her about meeting Dr. Henry Betts of the Rehabilitation Institute. She remembered visiting the Institute, and I went on to say that for eight years I had nurtured a dream of a tapestry designed by Chagall for Chicago. Then reported my conversation with Dr. Betts regarding a tapestry for the Institute.

I knew Vava was Chagall's business administrator, evaluating all new projects and encouraging him to embark on important ones, shaping his dreams into reality. Her voice would be the signal for a 'yes' or a 'no' to any request coming to Chagall. Vava simply said, "Why don't you ask him yourself? And with that, she left the room to tell Chagall we had arrived. I realized then that she approved of the idea of the commission.

There are moments in everyone's life that we never forget, magical moments. Such was July 9, 1982. Chagall walked in, full of vitality with flowing white hair, sparkling blue eyes, and had taken no more than ten steps when he pronounced in French, "The Bible is the greatest book every written." He sat down between Ralph and me. Knowing he preferred to speak Yiddish when we were alone, I continued his thought, "Speaking of the Bible, I have this wonderful idea. Would you design a tapestry based on the Bible for a hospital in Chicago that is dedicated to the healing of the disabled people of the world?"

After a few moments of consideration, Chagall's answer came not as a spoken 'no' or a 'yes'. With a nod of his head downward, his chin toward his chest, he signified his approval.

I had previously asked Dr. Betts to give me a reason why Chagall should accept the commission. He responded, "While doctors, medicine and surgery and an array of rehabilitation specialists and their technical skills can help a person to recover, it is the aesthetics of music and art that can give them hope and hasten the healing process, emotionally and physically."

That morning at La Colline, I relayed Dr. Betts' thoughts to Chagall. He replied with great enthusiasm and a wonderful smile, "Now I am a doctor!" And now the work would begin.

Chapter 11
The Job Tapestry: The Fulfillment

After all the excitement occasioned by our trip to France, a very frustrating year went by before the tangible work would begin on what would become Chagall's last major commission.

On our way home from St. Paul de Vence, Ralph and I stopped in Paris and met with Yvette Cauquil-Prince to tell her about the concept for the tapestry for the Rehabilitation Institute of Chicago, and to ask for her tentative agreement to take on this exciting project. Yvette Cauquil-Prince, an artist and master weaver, had worked with Picasso, Calder, Braque, Klee and Max Ernst, transforming their art into her own special medium. She had also collaborated with Chagall on thirty-three tapestries over a period of more than seventeen years. "Such a long association is based on trust, unlimited respect and faith and mutual compatibility and esteem," Yvette Cauquil-Prince commented. "In the case of Chagall, he was very rare, very sensitive, very tender." Chagall regarded Yvette as his "spiritual daughter."

Over the next thirteen months, the progress to bring a Chagall tapestry to Chicago inched forward. A carefully thought out plan to gain approval of the Institute's Board of Directors was put in place.

Of course, a piece of that strategy was to take Dr. Betts to Milwaukee to view the *Jeremiah* tapestry, and that was accomplished after two months of trying to fit it into his busy schedule. I went with him on that one-day trip, and we met with Ben Barkin, an advertising executive in Milwaukee, who was one of the people responsible for bringing the *Jeremiah* tapestry to the Helfaer Jewish Community Center. After viewing the stunning work, Dr. Betts' reaction was even more enthusiastic than when we had first discussed the project in France.

The Institute's Board of Directors, however, was less enthusiastic in its response when Dr. Betts recommended the commission of a Chagall tapestry. The matter was discussed at several board meetings, and each time, new objections and questions were raised. Fortunately, Eleanor Wood-Prince was a member of the Board; her voice was a most persuasive and positive force.

Finally, I believe what tipped the balance in the approval process was my meeting with the Board, in which I explained that the newly formed tapestry committee would not solicit contributions from any of the present or past donors to the Institute. Further, I pointed out that through the committee's efforts, we would be able to introduce a whole new group of contributors to the work of the Institute, whose names could be added to the regular list of donors.

Consequently, after seven months of discussion, the Board of Directors of the Rehabilitation Institute voted to accept the tapestry as a gift from the Friends of the Chagall Tapestry, as the committee would come to be known.

During the time when these preliminaries were carried out, Dr. Betts corresponded with Chagall. His letters indicated the connection he found between the work of the Institute and the artist. In part, he wrote, "…it would seem to me that your works, above all other artists, have the great aura of hope and faith. They convey the exhilaration of the world and the human spirit and of people's relationship to one another…I feel that you, better than anyone else in the world, could signify to my patients and to the people who come to visit them and to this large and supportive community, the philosophy that I feel."

In meantime, the word had spread about the committee that I was forming to bring a Chagall tapestry to Chicago. Starting with one person, it quickly grew to a committee of thirty-one members. It was definitely a Chagallian group of diverse people – crossing races, religions, ages and economic standings. It wasn't a select group; it was very open. Only two people on the committee had a connection to the Art Institute of Chicago or to the art world.

The guiding rule was to welcome participation from a broad spectrum of Chicagoans interested in the exciting project. This vision reflected both the universal appeal of the artist, and the diversity of the city. The group brought its collective experience to every aspect of the project: from negotiations to translations to administration, public relations, and fundraising.

When the committee, which I nicknamed "Camp Chagall," first met we didn't have one cent in the bank. The amount of money needed was $175,000. As I explained to Chagall, Yvette Cauquil-Prince, and to the various officials, the commission would have to be financed without a down payment and on an installment payment plan. Because the work was to be a gift for a hospital for rehabilitating the disabled and because of the broad make-up of the committee, the plan was accepted. With Chagall's advancing age, there was an urgency underlined in every discussion and decision.

Once we had received approval of the Institute's Board of Directors, work was started to complete the contracts for Chagall and Yvette. Also we had to measure and plot the dimensions of the lobby and the size of the tapestry.

Chagall had an innate perception concerning the use of any space in which his artwork was to be exhibited. He was actively involved in the planning of where and how his monumental works of art, like his mosaics, tapestries and stained glass windows, would be displayed. The proportions of height, length and width of the lobby and its surrounding space were vitally important to him, and his age of ninety-six did not deter him from telling people where and how he wanted to handle a project.

For instance, *The Four Seasons* mosaic was initially planned to be a one dimensional mosaic, located on a wall below the first level of the First National Bank in Chicago. Chagall vetoed that idea. He recommended that the mosaic be a much larger work for the enormous plaza before the bank's main entrance. It would be a work that people could walk around and experience the change in the seasons in a perfect sunlit setting.

For the windows at the synagogue of the Hadassah Hospital in Israel, a model of the hospital was shown to Chagall. He was quite upset when he saw the actual space that was allotted to his glorious windows, feeling that the building was too small to house the windows properly.

Consequently, when planning the tapestry at the Institute, and understanding Chagall's interest and feeling for space in relation to the actual artwork, I wanted to ensure that a suitable setting was provided for the tapestry. Pierre Provoyeur, the curator of the Chagall Biblical Museum in France, happened to be in New York during the planning process, so I asked him to come to Chicago and consult with the architects of the Institute.

Meticulous measurements were taken, and schematic drawings were produced to provide Chagall with a comprehensive understanding of the ceiling height and distances between walls in the lobby, with all notations made in French. We developed the idea of a horizontal tapestry. We even had some sketches drawn showing its placement in the lobby of the Institute sent to Chagall.

Even before the contracts were finalized, I knew that the tapestry had to be based on a Biblical theme. Consulting a Biblical concordance, I settled on verse seven from the fourteenth chapter of *Job*. Coincidentally, a young physician on Dr. Betts' staff had asked his rabbi, for a recommendation and the rabbi had chosen the same verse.

> *"For there is hope of a tree,*
> *If it be cut down, that it will sprout again,*
> *And that the tender branch thereof will not cease."*

The verse was sent to Chagall, and we had suggested bright colors of red, yellow and orange. We also recommended that the Tree of Life be included, since it was a symbol of the Institute. Finally, the suggestion was made that the horizontal tapestry have measurements of a height of 10 feet and a width of 13 to 15 feet.

At this point, an unforeseen obstacle almost brought the project to a crashing halt. It occurred when Vava reviewed with Chagall the three ideas that the committee and the Institute's Board of Directors had proposed as a wish list to be included in the tapestry.

Exactly one week after submitting the ideas in writing, Vava called to tell me that the project had to be cancelled, because Chagall wanted to decline the commission. Others might have accepted the decision, thinking that an artist of 95 years of age had simply changed his mind.

But not Vivian Jacobson! I was brought up under the watchful eye of my mother's sister, my Aunt Gertrude, a powerful woman, who taught me to distinguish between the two uses of the word 'no'. On the one hand, 'no' was a selfish word, with negative connotations. On the other hand, 'no' was a word of love and of concern. To Aunt Gertrude and to Vava Chagall, it meant that an idea was wrong, or not good enough, and that it could be made better.

So, when Vava told me no, I asked her, "What can we do to continue with the tapestry project? Is there something that needs to be changed or reorganized or improved? Perhaps we can correct the problems. What are Chagall's wishes?"

Chagall's wishes were for a tapestry to be created in blues and greens, the colors of hope. He had said, "There is no hope in red, yellow and orange." Secondly, although the tree is a symbol of life, the reference to the tree had already been made in the biblical citation, and Chagall thought that people need people when they are disabled. Therefore the configurations would center on Job and his wife.

Lastly, Vava reported that Chagall was very dismayed by the presentation of a horizontal tapestry. As in the original color choices, Chagall had said, "There is no hope in horizontal." He wanted the dimensions turned around to a new direction, 13 feet in height and 10 feet in width. "It should hang from the ceiling, so that when the patients are in the lobby in their wheelchairs, they can look up with their eyes following to the heavens and be with God." I thought this statement to be brilliant.

Chagall's wishes were acknowledged and agreed upon. I told Vava that the tapestry would be hung facing eastward towards Jerusalem, an idea that pleased Chagall. The project was back on track.

Some weeks later, I made arrangements to fly to Europe to present the final contracts, and to open the bank accounts in Switzerland and Paris to which the installment payments were to be made. Of course, in preparation for the trip, I picked up a box of Chagall's favorite Frango Mints from Marshall Fields, and Ralph gave me a delicate sterling silver spoon with a tiny bird on the top that he had found for Chagall.

In making the flight reservations in business class on Air France, I had made a special request that if possible, I would like a seat with an empty seat beside me, since I would need extra room to review the contents of a large briefcase full of contracts during the flight. My request was granted. I had an aisle seat. Next to me was an empty middle seat, and the window seat was occupied by a gentleman.

While we exchanged pleasantries, he questioned, "To what do we owe this empty seat on such a crowded plane?" I told him about the purpose of my journey, mentioning that I had to start looking over the contracts immediately.

The man then introduced himself as an attorney, who specialized in the preparation of legal documents for clients in the United States and France. He offered to help me by reviewing the contracts. He explained the French legal system is quite different than ours, and sometimes contracts that are written by American attorneys are done so without the French legal system in mind.

He added that since his firm didn't allow him to do any pro bono work, we would have to keep his assistance a matter between the two of us. He explained that his wife is an art teacher fascinated by the work of Marc Chagall. She would be terribly disappointed if I didn't help you.

Suddenly there was another Chagall angel in my life, methodically reviewing the contracts as if they applied to a multi-million dollar deal on behalf of an American client doing business in France. He read with pencil in hand, making corrections, and fully explaining the reason for each correction.

This latest Chagall angel in the window seat also gave me the telephone number where he was staying in Lyon, should any problem arise during the signing of the contracts. As it turned out, the whole signing process was accomplished in no time, with no questions asked by either Chagall or Yvette.

As a measure of the trust and the hope with which Chagall greeted the project, even before the contracts were signed, he had begun work on the gouache, a drawing on which the tapestry was based.

The figure of Job floats in the right foreground, with his wife offering succor in the form of a flask of water. To the left is a large body of people and a representation of Jerusalem is in the background. The Christ configuration is in the top left hand corner. Typical Chagall animals and an angel carrying a Torah scroll round out the principal elements in this intricate composition.

The dream was no longer an illusion; it was fast approaching reality. On two occasions while he was working on the drawing, members of the committee and I went to France to meet with Chagall.

Yvette traveled from Paris to Chagall's home on repeated occasions to carry out their collaboration, and to decide about colors and the textures of the wool to be used in the tapestry. She saw her role "as an interpreter, capturing the spirit of the artist, much as a symphony orchestra conductor brings a composer to an audience."

Starting with the artist's design, she made a cartoon, an original drawing, in the final dimensions of the tapestry. This cartoon was a reversed drawing that contained her own special code. The code indicated the exact yarn mixes, the direction of the weaving itself (horizontal, curved or diagonal) and the color shadings chosen to interpret the original work.

"Chagall's art necessitated a particularly elaborate technique," commented Yvette Cauquil-Prince. "Job was created from an original gouache and executed on a low-warp, horizontal loom. Because it was worked on the reverse side, the front of the tapestry could not be seen during its creation."

In creating the tapestry, Yvette used three different kinds of wool from France, Australia and Scotland, all dyed specifically to Chagall's requirements. The work was woven in a combination of Coptic and medieval techniques, along rather than across the lines that mark the various colored areas,

On this side of the Atlantic, the committee was deep into the work of raising funds. Many methods were utilized to gather donations, such as direct mailings, personal visits and the sale of raffle tickets for a trip to France.

Fund raising events were held, including two benefits by the Hubbard Street Dance Company, the opening of Cartier, a new jewelry store on Michigan Avenue, and a showing of the Oscar de la Renta fall collection at Saks Fifth Avenue. At benefit cocktail parties we auctioned off such special treasures as a bottle of 1911 Moet-Chandon champagne, donated to us by the renowned wine maker, and a Chagall aquatint, donated by Gérald Cramer, Chagall's book editor from Switzerland.

The committee's efforts were enhanced by the corporate participation. First and foremost was the support of the Sara Lee Corporation, whose Chairman and CEO, John H. Bryan, Jr., became the Honorary Chair of the Friends of the Chagall Tapestry Committee.

Through John Bryan and with the assistance of vice-president Robert Lauer, who worked directly with the committee, we received generous backing and encouragement. In addition to a major corporate contribution, a number of luncheons, cocktail parties, and other special events were funded, the booklets for the dedication were underwritten, and staff assistance from legal and marketing departments was provided.

In all, 576 individual, corporate and foundation contributions were received. The donations came from twenty-two different states and from eleven countries throughout the world.

The committee received excellent publicity on its work from a number of regional and nationally recognized magazines and newspapers. An article in *The Chicago Tribune*, published early in 1985, resulted in my receiving a call from Charlene Breedlove of *The Journal of the American Medical Association* or JAMA, as it is popularly known. The magazine has a tradition of including reproductions of works of art on its covers, and they wished to feature the tapestry on the cover the week of the dedication.

When I relayed the request to Vava, the initial response was negative. Chagall didn't see why he should allow his work to be on the cover of a medical magazine. I met with Charlene and explained the problem. It was her idea to gather up past issues of JAMA with covers by Durer, El Greco, Rembrandt (whose work Chagall admired greatly and whom he often called his teacher), and other famous artists, and make the covers available for me to show Chagall on my next visit.

With that information in hand, the 'no' became a 'yes,' and Vava said it was not necessary to bring the actual magazines. Consequently, the issue of JAMA June 20, 1986 – the date on which the tapestry was dedicated – carried a picture of the tapestry on its cover, together with an accompanying story, with comments by Dr. Betts regarding the arts as imperative for the healing process. This was the first of what would be many Chagall covers featured on JAMA.

Meanwhile, in February 1985, I met with Chagall at his home. The tapestry was about eighty percent completed at that time. Although Chagall appeared to be more frail than at any time I had seen him previously, he was looking forward to seeing the finished work. A month later he died, without having seen his final superb vision of hope for the world.

When the tapestry was finished, at Vava's request, I made another trip to Paris to see this remarkable and moving piece. Little did I realize when I stood in Yvette's studio on that day that the next nine months would be filled with one agonizing frustration after another as I tried to have the tapestry delivered to Chicago.

Not only was the delivery of the tapestry to the Rehabilitation Institute held up by the legal aspects of settling Marc Chagall's estate, but the Republic of France had very firm objections to the tapestry leaving the country.

I cannot accurately describe the exasperation and annoyance I felt as each day passed without a solution. I considered holding a news conference, I made innumerable telephone calls abroad to anyone who I thought could break the logjam, I wrote countless letters, some with a somewhat hostile tone, I admit. Finally, the legal and custodial difficulties were settled with assistance from France's consul-general in Chicago, a vice president of the Banque National de Paris based in Chicago, and with two attorneys from our committee, Elizabeth Ragan, an outstanding international tax lawyer and Ralph.

Finally, on a spring day in 1986, Swissair arrived at O'Hare Airport, with the tapestry in a small metal trunk. It had a very flimsy lock. I was accompanied by Don Olson, the Director of Education for the Rehabilitation Institute, who had spent many hours and much effort on the project. Don had served as a liaison between our committee and the Board of Directors, and his help had been invaluable.

I had arranged for a team from a company that specialized in packing and shipping of paintings to meet us at the airport. They brought all sorts of tools with them, which were of course unnecessary. Don and I stood dumbfounded, looking at the way this tapestry, which had been insured for 1,500,000 French francs, had been prepared for shipment. The tapestry, weighing seventy-five pounds, had merely been folded, pushed into an old trunk and sent on its way.

Don Olson expressed his reaction, "My thought at seeing the trunk was one of disappointment. I wondered how it could hold the large art work that I was expecting. As the tapestry was rolled out, each fold revealed a mass of color, design and beauty. I had chills of excitement with each roll revealing more and more of the wonderful work."

At first, some members of the Board of Directors of the Art Institute of Chicago had been reluctant about the placement of a Chagall work in a non-museum setting, such as the Rehabilitation Institute. However, by the time the tapestry arrived all objections were overcome, and the staff of the Art Institute proved to be of immeasurable assistance. They provided supervisory advice on how the tapestry should displayed. Proper lighting was critical. They sent personnel do the work and to deal with such matters as air conditioning and heating all at no expense to the Rehabilitation Institute.

June 20, 1986 was the day chosen for the formal unveiling and presentation of the *Job* tapestry to the Rehabilitation Institute. A full day's schedule of events began with a breakfast and a showing to patients, their families and selected close friends and staff. Then the formal ceremony followed with Vava Chagall, Yvette Cauquil-Prince and Chagall's granddaughter, Bella Meyer, in attendance for the unveiling.

Other events were a luncheon, an afternoon reception for members of the art and medical communities, including contributors, and a dinner honoring the members of our committee. In the days following the formal unveiling, a chamber music concert was held in memory of Chagall, and a seminar was given by five theologians on an overview of the Book of Job.

So much of the time that I had spent on the project had taken place at the Institute itself, and I had grown to appreciate the warmth and the compassionate atmosphere and the devotion of the staff members. I marveled at the determination and the resolve of the patients themselves in the face of what must have seemed in many cases like insurmountable obstacles. I had eaten with them in the cafeteria, visited with them in the hallways and on the elevators, and talked with their families on many occasions. So, when I gave my remarks at the dedication on the morning of June 20th, I spoke to the patients from my heart.

"This tapestry is our gift to you. Your gift to us has been your courage, your perseverance and commitment to a better and more productive life. You have inspired us....And our friend, Marc Chagall, leaves us this spiritual message, 'But in Art, as in life, everything is possible, so long as it is based on love.'"

When I consider the four years that it took to complete the tapestry project, I realized that, although some people may have thought me crazy to have the idea of commissioning a tapestry, those who knew me and who worked with me on the project went along with my dream. For this I say, "Only the idealists make reality happen for the realists."

A short time after Chagall's death, I received a letter from Vava Chagall stating her happiness with the completed tapestry. This is an excerpt from that letter:

Chere Amie
J'ai vu la tapisserie que Mme Cauquil-Prince a faite. Elle est trés, trés belle. Je pense qu'elle est une des plus belles qu'elle ait jamais réalisée jusqu'a maintenant.

Vava Chagall

Dear Friend
I saw the tapestry that Mme Cauquil-Prince made. It is very, very beautiful. I think it is the most beautiful that she has ever realized until now.

Vava Chagall

Chapter 12
A Farewell

On February 22, 1985 I visited Chagall for what was to be the last time. The *Job* tapestry, being woven in Paris, was near completion. I brought two presents for Chagall – his chocolate candies and a book of three plays by Shakespeare, translated into Yiddish. Ralph had found the book while browsing in a second-hand store and purchased it immediately, knowing of Chagall's love of the theater and the Yiddish language.

As the time came for me to leave, I went to say goodbye to him and found him reading from the book that I had brought and eating his chocolates. It was a poignant moment.

Five weeks later on March 28, (the Hebrew date the 6th of Nisan 5745), I received a phone call that Chagall had passed away very quietly in the evening. The news of his passing was on every radio and television station as the world mourned their loss. Our telephone rang constantly with people wanting to express their condolences. Even the BBC called from London for a telephone interview.

Passover was only three days away. How could I leave to go to France for the funeral that was to be on Monday, first of April? Ralph helped me to understand that I must go. He would make the Passover without me. However, getting there at first seemed to be impossible. Easter and Passover had come together on that weekend. There was not a seat available on any airline.

Thanks to the ingenuity of my travel agent, Marc Berkman, I was able to leave on Saturday, March 30. Berkman had called several European airlines to see if they had a frequent flier client who would be willing to give up a seat for me and travel the following day. Swissair had called him back two hours later and told him that they had a Zurich business traveler who would be happy to give up his place so that I could attend the funeral of Marc Chagall.

Swissair booked me on a flight to Zurich with a connection to Nice. I arrived at O'Hare Airport, picked up my ticket, and went to the gate area. While I was waiting, a gentleman approached me and asked if I was the person who had been interviewed by the local NBC television station on the passing of Marc Chagall. I said I was, and with that he introduced himself and his wife and offered their condolences.

Our conversation was overheard by other passengers in the waiting area and soon there was a small group of us discussing the attributes of Chagall as an artist and as a person. I was not alone in my sorrow, as strangers became friends during the time waiting for the plane to depart.

About a half hour before we arrived in Zurich, I realized that in my haste to pack and get ready to leave, I hadn't had time to visit a salon to have my hair washed and trimmed and to get a manicure. And I knew that once I arrived in Nice, there wouldn't be any time to make myself presentable for the funeral.

I asked the flight attendant if it would be possible for me to go into Zurich when we landed, find a salon, and get back to the airport in the 3 1/2 hour layover time until the scheduled flight to Nice. She said she would consult with the pilot since she thought there was a beauty shop in Terminal 2 in the Zurich airport.

The flight attendant returned several minutes later and reported that the pilot had called the terminal beauty shop and explained that I was on my way to Chagall's funeral and needed an immediate appointment upon arrival. I thought to myself that this pilot is supposed to be flying an airplane and preparing for a landing, and here he is making a beauty shop appointment for me.

The power of having Chagall as a friend once again was demonstrated as a problem solver. Chagall angels were everywhere, including in the cockpit of a Swissair plane.

When the plane landed, an airline representative directed me to the quickest route to Terminal 2, the large salon which was patronized mainly by airline personnel. A hairdresser stood at the entrance, waiting for me, scissors and cape in hand. In no time I had my hair and nails done. I even had time to spare to have some lunch and make my connecting flight to Nice without any problem at all.

Actually, Chagall angels were at work every step of my journey - the travel agent who made a special effort to find me a flight, a business man that gave up his seat for me, a group of people discussing the art and the mind of Chagall in O'Hare Airport as a tribute to his passing. Then the flight attendant and pilot, as well as the hairdresser and manicurist, made it possible for me to look my best. Who can doubt the influence of the angels of Chagall?

I arrived late in the day at the Hotel Le Hameau in St. Paul de Vence, where I always stayed while visiting Chagall. I found that so many dignitaries from Chagall's world who had arrived for the funeral, that my room had been given to Ida Chagall. However, to resolve the situation, the staff of the museum had arranged for a local woman to open her home to people who could not find a hotel room.

The staff thought this would be a lovely place for me, because it had an outdoor swimming pool. No matter that it was the end of March and the temperature was very chilly, their thoughts were definitely in the right place.

My hostess, who was pleased to have me as her guest, served me a delicious dinner. Afterwards, I quickly fell asleep, exhausted from traveling and from the emotional stress preparing for the funeral.

There was no doubt in my mind what I would wear for the solemn occasion. I had worn a black suit when I was interviewed by the local television station the day after Chagall's passing, but I knew I was not going to wear black for the funeral. I chose color, lots of color, bright beautiful colors to honor my friend.

I wore a red silk suit with a soft yellow blouse. My coat was a powder blue, my beret was a light chartreuse. And my scarf was an Oscar de la Renta, a gift from my neighbor, done in marvelous hues of blue, aqua, orange, yellow and pink with a design of butterflies imprinted on the material.

When I arrived at the cemetery, I stood out, as everyone was dressed in somber grays, browns and black. The following morning, the *Nice Matin* newspaper printed a picture of Chagall's funeral. The photo was taken from a distance, capturing the number of mourners that were there. I alone provided the only contrast in the photo that was published in color.

Charles Sorlier, the lithographer and close associate of Chagall, wrote the essay "In Memoriam," which appears in the book, *Chagall, A Retrospective*, edited by Jacob Baal-Teshuva, a part of which describes that day, April 1, 1985.

"On the morning of the funeral, the little village of Saint-Paul was invaded by a crowd. The sky had dressed in Chagall blue in honor of the event. Busloads of tourists, so numerous during the Easter season, brought a flood of visitors – German, Japanese, Italian and American – a mixture of races to attend the ceremony, as though achieving the Universal Brotherhood which meant so much to the Master.

The shopkeepers paid homage to him all along his final route by hanging reproductions of his work in their windows. Family members and guests of honor were to be cordoned off from the crowds by the police, but they were overcome by a human wave impossible to contain. I was not able to gain entry to the tiny cemetery. There the lowliest peasant rubbed elbows with the high and mighty to accompany Chagall to his eternal reward. He is very happy.

I did not use the wrong verb tense in the above sentence, for only those with barren minds can believe that the Master is dead. He is simply walking around this world in the state of levitation which was peculiar to him."

The funeral took place in the municipal cemetery in St. Paul de Vence. This village was Chagall's home for many years with Vava.

Standing next to me during the ceremony was Eleanor Wood-Prince on one side, and Evelyn Nef on the other side. Mrs. Nef and her husband, John, a professor at the University of Chicago, had been close friends of the Chagalls.

As we were waiting for the short memorial service to begin, which was to be conducted by Jacques Lang, the Minister of Culture, I was approached by an elderly gentleman who had been walking around like a wandering Jew in the cemetery. He was Leon Leneman, the president of the Jewish writers and journalists of France, and an old friend of Chagall.

Speaking in Yiddish, Leneman asked me if I would recite the Kaddish with him, and asked if any of the other Jews present. The only ones, whom I knew personally, aside from members of Chagall's family, were Ovadia Soffer, the Ambassador from Israel to France, and Professor Bernstein from the mathematics department at the University of Nice.

As the casket began to be lowered into the ground, Leneman walked up to the coffin in his very long grey coat and held up his hands to halt the ceremony. Piet, the son of Ida, gave permission for the saying of the Kaddish. Then in this very heartrending moment, he and I, joined by Ambassador Soffer and Professor Bernstein, began to recite the somber prayer. There are no words in any language to express what it is like for a Jew to say the Kaddish, the holiest of prayers, in these surroundings.

In such a setting, Leneman's deep voice resounded out to those attending the service and to the surrounding area. He had the last word, for he insisted that his dear friend Chagall would be buried with the recitation of the Kaddish, this holy Jewish prayer. I will always remember Leon Leneman.

Several years passed before I visited Chagall's home in Vitebsk, in 1997. I carefully selected three stones from the backyard of his renovated childhood home. Unlike people from other religions, Jews do not typically place flowers at gravesites. Instead they often place stones on the grave or tombstone. The origin of the custom is uncertain, but the most common explanation is that placing stones is a symbolic act that indicates someone has come to visit and the deceased has not been forgotten.

I wanted to have these stones from Vitebsk to place on the gravesite of Chagall at some future time. In the meantime, I gave one of them to Klaus Mayer, the parish priest at St. Stephan Church in Mainz, Germany when I visited him a year later.

When I once again returned to France, I stood at the gravesite of Chagall in St. Paul de Vence. With great reverence I placed one of the stones on the marker, keeping the third stone as a worshipful reminder. I stepped back, recited the Kaddish and cried. I miss my friend.

Some people give so much to the world while they are living that when they are no longer on this earth, they continue to live on. This is the legacy of Marc Chagall.

Chapter 13
Moving Forward

Thirty-eight years have passed since I gave my first lecture on Chagall to the Women's Auxiliary Board of the Michael Reese Hospital of Chicago. The invitation to speak to the group came from Rose Goldman. She and her husband, Morris, were well-known art patrons, and she knew of my appointment as President of the American Friends of the Chagall Biblical Message Museum. Although I had never given a lecture on Chagall, I was intrigued by the idea of presenting a talk about my friend, the artist.

I relied on the presentation of the two documentary films by Chuck Olin – *The Gift*, the story of *The Four Seasons* mosaic in downtown Chicago and *The Palette of Glass*, an account of the creation of the *America Windows* at the Art Institute of Chicago. In this way, I could let Chagall speak for himself, since in the films he comments on the creative process, art, music, and life in general.

A few introductory and closing remarks, and a short question and answer session, completed my fledgling attempt to present Chagall to an audience. However, somewhat to my surprise, the group was delighted, and my career as a Chagall lecturer was launched.

Over time I have developed fourteen lectures on various aspects of Chagall's life and his major artworks. In doing the necessary research and reading for each lecture, I have found that there is no end to Chagall – his life, his work, his dreams, and his charismatic personality. Few people know who I am, but they know the name "Chagall," and his creations serve as a magnet, drawing rooms full of people wanting to hear about the artist who so obviously brought so much joy and wonder into their lives.

Although I had given many lectures on Chagall in Chicago and abroad, the impetus for a busy schedule was established once we moved to North Carolina. At first, I gave several different lectures for the Arts Council of Moore County, and at the Weymouth Center for the Arts and Humanities, both located in Southern Pines.

Then in 1998, I applied to become a speaker for the North Carolina Humanities Council, for a program that is now called the "Roads Scholars Speakers Bureau" which offers a wide variety of subjects by knowledgeable speakers throughout the state. I was honored to be chosen as a speaker. What better way to spread the message of Marc Chagall?

An interesting observation about my reception as a lecturer in North Carolina is that it often is more enthusiastic, because of my credentials as an athlete. Strange as it may sound, my years of experience as a swimmer, as a swimming instructor/trainer and a director of waterfronts in various national and international locations, appear to give me special recognition in this sports-loving state.

I bring my PowerPoint presentation, my knowledge, energy, and enthusiasm about Chagall to churches, synagogues, schools, universities, art galleries, museums, and other groups ranging from twenty to four hundred people. Aside from appearing in North Carolina, I have brought the Chagall message to people in twenty-one other states, Europe and Israel, and I even gave a lecture at a reunion of the wonderful summer camp in Wisconsin that I attended over seventy years ago.

After each lecture, someone is always ready to tell a story that relates to the artist in some way. Some of these stories are meant to be shared!

One day after a lecture on Chagall's European stained glass windows, a woman approached me, with great anger. It developed that she had just returned from a bus tour in Switzerland, and while in Zurich, the tour bus had passed the Fraumünster church that had beautiful Chagall windows. But the tour leader said in an off-hand manner that they wouldn't have time to stop to view the windows – they weren't that important! After the woman had seen my slides, she was very upset that the tour leader had bypassed the windows.

We exchanged cards, and I commiserated with her. She later wrote me that she had called her travel agent and complained so forcefully that the agent sent her a check of $250 and a letter of apology.

One afternoon my lecture was interrupted by an emergency call for a woman in the audience. She immediately left, and I learned later that her husband had been rushed to the hospital with a heart attack. Ten months later I gave a lecture in a neighboring community. At the reception following the event, a woman and her husband came up to speak with me. This was the woman who had to leave because of her husband's sudden illness.

The husband explained, "When we heard you were scheduled to speak, we wanted to come. I was advised very forcefully, I should not take ill again while you are giving your lecture. She said she would not leave for a second time under any circumstances." I laughed with them, thanked them for coming, and wished them both continued good health.

I was invited to give a lecture and slide presentation to a 5th and 6th grade art class in West End, North Carolina. I discussed the excitement of viewing a Chagall painting and how to have a conversation with the artist based on the viewer's experience in his/her own life. One of the slides that I showed from the Bible series was *Abraham and the Three Angels*. When the presentation was finished I asked the students if there were any questions. One hand went up immediately. A young man asked, "Why did that man (Chagall) paint Abraham's face in so many different colors of green, blue, red, orange, and yellow?" I did not have the answer to the question, but told him that I will do the research. If there is an answer, I will send it to him in the mail.

As soon as I finished, another young man was jumping up and down with his hand waving vigorously. He shouted, "I have the answer, I have the answer! The man who painted that picture did it that way because Abraham was the father of all people. If he would have painted his face one color then that would mean that he was the father of only one people." This is one of the most inspirational statements I ever heard in any of my lectures. If Chagall was in the room he would have taken this young man's head into his loving hands and looking into his face with a gentile smile would have said, "Vous comprenez Chagall."

On another occasion, a man arrived with a nurse, his daughter, his wife, a wheelchair and an oxygen tank, and insisted on a front row seat. The wife quietly said that her husband was terminally ill, but had been a great admirer of Chagall forever, and he was adamant about coming to hear me speak despite his physical condition.

I gave the lecture my all, knowing how important it was for him. To this day, I recall his hanging on every word, and remember the determined spirit of this man to make the effort to come and hear my Chagall lecture. I subsequently found out that he died just a few days later.

Florence, South Carolina, would appear to be the last place to find a missing piece of a puzzle regarding Vava Chagall. I had often wondered if Vava had ever been married prior to her meeting Chagall, and I had never been able to find the answer. Then after a lecture in Florence, a very distinguished older woman told me that her uncle was married to Vava for three years in London.

The statement took my breath away. The woman continued to tell the story of her mother's brother, Russian-born, who was a widower with two small children living in London in the 1920s when he married Vava. The marriage was short-lived because Vava apparently didn't have a good relationship with the children, according to the story-teller. I have since tried unsuccessfully to confirm all the facts of the marriage, but no mention of it is contained in any of the voluminous writings about Chagall.

The question and answer sessions with which I conclude each of my lectures are always interesting. Two of the questions I am frequently asked:

- How did you meet Chagall?
- Why does Chagall paint all those floating figures and animals?

And some of the more unusual questions:

- Did Chagall have different periods of painting, like Picasso?
- Have you heard Aaron Copland's musical composition on Vitebsk?
- Have you seen Chagall's painting at Tossa del Mar, north of Barcelona, Spain?

For answers to these questions and many others, please come to one of my lectures.

August 2003 was a milestone on the path of my lecture series. Until that time, I had focused on ten different presentations about Chagall, his life and his work. That summer I renewed an old friendship with Jerry Weinstein at a first decade Camp Ramah reunion, and he introduced me to two thoughtful works by author Peter Guralnick on Elvis Presley.

I was always a longtime fan of Elvis Presley, and ten years earlier I embarked on a worldwide adventure to hand out United States postage stamps bearing the likeness of Elvis. The stamps were issued on January 8, 1993. I gave the stamps to friends and strangers whom I met in my travels during the next four years and in return, always received a reaction of overwhelming gratitude and delight from the recipients.

Later that summer Jerry sent me a copy of the Guralnick book, *Last Train from Memphis*, and the companion work by the same author, *Careless Love: The Unmaking of Elvis Presley*. My reading schedule for the next few weeks was set.

At the time I had been reading Benjamin Harshav's definitive biography,

Marc Chagall and His Times: A Documentary Narrative. Now I began a regimen of reading 100 pages of Guralnick on Presley, and then alternating with 100 pages of Harshav on Chagall.

I noted the remarkable parallels between the artist and the singer. Their great passion for their music and art gave them a commonality. Although no real connection existed between the two, in many ways they were alike in their pursuit of excellence. As I read, a gem of an idea took shape. What about preparing a new lecture comparing these two 20th century icons?

The more I thought about doing a lecture on Chagall and Elvis, the more energized I became. The phone calls and e-mails between my computer and Jerry Weinstein's multiplied as we discussed the pros and cons of the project. I had previously sent him a copy of my favorite book on Chagall, and also a story that I had written about my Elvis stamp campaign.

I welcomed Jerry's insightful and interesting comments. After all, it turned out he was an attorney, like Ralph! And now I had, not one, but two, individuals who believed in me and what I was trying to accomplish.

As this eleventh lecture drew near, I became increasingly stimulated by its prospects. I was astonished that the passion of Chagall and Elvis brought me more enthusiasm than any other adventure I had ever attempted. I found a new abundance of energy, my health was great, and my mind was clear and sharp, open to every nuance and every possibility as I compared these celebrated artists.

The introduction to the lecture set the tone. I recalled hearing a television interview of a Middle East peace negotiator at a Geneva, Switzerland Peace Conference, who said that if opposing factions would go in a room and talk about what they have in common, rather than emphasizing their differences, most peace talks would be successful.

The concept of commonality that applies to family, friends, our community and the world is one that brought the lives of Chagall and Elvis into focus for me. The fervor of Chagall's paintings and the energy of Elvis' music fused together as I studied and did research for the lecture.

The two men shared a deep respect for religion; both of them were born into the humblest of circumstances in out of the way places, and both had mothers who had confidence in them and trust in their early childhood talents. Their mothers did everything possible to provide the paints and paper, the piano and guitar for their sons, respectively. Above all, Chagall and Elvis were true to their art form. For instance, Chagall maintained the highest standards for all of his work, as did Elvis in choosing his back-up musicians carefully, and his recording sessions weren't over until the sound was absolutely right.

I used a multi-media approach for the Chagall-Presley lecture, interweaving slides of Chagall's famous paintings with recordings of Elvis' most popular numbers. For several years I dreamed about adding original music to the lecture series. The inspiration came from Chagall himself, a great lover of music. And it was a natural consequence since one of his hopes was that the integration of music and art would contribute to world peace. But I wanted something more than recordings for the Chagall-Presley lecture.

The search for a composer who could create a piece of music that would enhance the lecture presentation, and one of whom Chagall would approve, took the better part of a year. Early on in my quest, I found a likely candidate, Seth Weinstein, the son of my friend, Jerry.

I learned that Seth was a multi-talented musician and graduate of Harvard University, whose background included more than ten years of classical piano, theory and composition studies. Now based in New York City, Seth worked extensively in the theater world as a pianist/keyboardist, musical director, conductor and composer.

I had to wait to meet him, though, because at the time of my discovery, Seth was touring Europe as a pianist for a musical production of *Fosse*. In the meantime, the lecture, *Elvis and Chagall*, was unveiled in the warm and relaxed setting of The Country Bookshop in Southern Pines, to a capacity audience of sixty people.

The audience response to the lecture was amazing. The artistic beauty of the Chagall slides and the recorded music of Elvis proved to be a winning combination, such as in Elvis' rendition of *The Wonder of You* in conjunction with a slide of Chagall's *Lovers in the Moonlight*.

The best part of the evening, however, came when I presented slides of the *White Crucifixion* and other paintings of the Christ configuration of the crucifixion and resurrection, together with stained glass windows from European churches and cathedrals. I matched these beautiful works of Chagall with a recording of Elvis singing *Amazing Grace*. After about a minute, I asked the audience if they would like to sing along, and sing they did, with every ounce of their individual spiritual beings. It was a breathtaking experience!

The next several months flew by, as I explored ways to expand the Chagall-Presley lecture, and attempted to bring it to the attention of several New York and Memphis contacts, all the while continuing my search for a composer. And of course, I pursued my regular lecture schedule.

One of those programs was in Sedona, Arizona, where I spoke on *Chagall and the Women in His Life*. During the same trip, Ralph gave two lectures on the Holocaust and his life in Germany as a child. After my talk, a woman introduced herself as Ceil Blumen and told me that she and her husband would be our hosts for dinner the next night.

Ceil Blumen went on to say that she too was from Chicago, and had graduated with me from Senn High School. I took another look and I realized I was talking to a former classmate, Ceil Katz. We laughed about having found each other after all these years.

Upon meeting her husband, a physician, the next evening, I noted he had a deep Southern drawl, and I asked where he was from originally. The answer – Memphis! I put down my fork and stopped eating. I had been trying to make a Memphis connection for several months. I knew more people in Paris, France, than I did in all of Tennessee. Now sitting right across from me was a Memphis native.

As I explained to the Blumens, I would very much like to give my Chagall-Elvis lecture in Memphis, but had no viable personal contacts. Dr. Blumen told me that his brother went to high school with Elvis, and he knew George Klein, one of Elvis' closest friends. More importantly, he gave me the name and telephone number of a highly placed individual in Memphis who would be the number one contact for me. You see, you can even have dinner with a Chagall angel in Sedona, Arizona.

Needless to say, his contact, Herb Notowich, was successful in making arrangements for me to appear the following August during the week long celebration of the anniversary of Elvis' death at The Dixon Gallery and Gardens, one of Memphis' premier art museums. Now the time had come to make a final decision about the selection of the composer for the piece of music that I definitely wanted to accompany the Memphis presentation.

I had conducted lengthy telephone interviews with a number of composers and had listened carefully to recordings of their works. But I had also met Seth Weinstein and was impressed with his quiet manner, his love of life, his adventurous charm, and his classical musical background.

In my imagination, I brought Chagall and Seth together. They are in Chagall's home in St. Paul de Vence, and Seth is sitting at the piano, playing a Mozart sonata for Chagall. They smile at one another, and Chagall gives his famous nod. At that point, the decision was made! Early in 2005, Seth and I collaborated on a piece called, simply, *Conversations*.

I say we collaborated, but in actuality, my part in the composition was to give Seth a crash course on Chagall – his life and his loves and his immeasurable talent. To a lesser extent, I supplied him with written material detailing Elvis' upbringing and lifestyle, as well as films, CDs and recordings of The King of Rock and Roll, demonstrating his musical range from gospel to ballads to country and rock and roll.

Seth had begun his composing career while still at Harvard, adapting Judith Guest's novel *Ordinary People* as a full-length musical production. His creativity had also resulted in the composition of four musical comedies. He took to our partnership with enthusiasm, eagerly cramming a lot of knowledge into a short space of time.

As Seth worked on the project, his understanding of the two icons increased. "I never listened to rock when I was growing up, and didn't know much about The King," he told me. In composing the piece, Weinstein started with Chagall because he came first chronologically. He began it with a classical theme that has Russian overtones. The music then segues into a slow beat of traditional Jewish tunes that grow faster as it transforms into a rock style. For a while, the piece belongs to the King, then it is a combination that reflects the two artists, and finally it closes with the original Russian-style theme infused with an Elvis-style pop beat.

Conversations is eleven minutes in length and is meant to serve as a solo piece. However, for the Memphis performance as Seth and I worked together prior to its premiere, it became an integral part of the lecture. It was used first as an overture, then familiar themes were brought back and interwoven with melodic elements illustrating sections of my talk, and the music was reprised in a dramatic conclusion.

Before the appearance in Memphis, Seth spent several days at the Weymouth Center for the Arts and Humanities, under the Center's Artist-in-Residence program, putting the finishing touches on *Conversations*. It was a joy to work with him and watch him as he fine-tuned a passage in the composition. Always receptive to my suggestions, he was a Chagallian artist in his own right.

We gave a dress rehearsal program at the Weymouth Center at the conclusion of Seth's Artist-in-Residence week, and it went beautifully, with encore after encore requested by the audience. The lecture, with the approval of the Elvis Presley Enterprises, at The Dixon Gallery and Gardens, co-sponsored by the Bornblum Center for Judaic Studies at the University of Memphis, was truly the highlight of my lecture series that year.

To appear in the elegant surroundings of The Dixon Gallery with its fine permanent collection of French Impressionists and superb gardens was a special occasion. It was standing-room only for well over 325 attendees. Seth and I received an enthusiastic standing ovation.

To make the event even more exciting, after our presentation of the Chagall and Elvis lecture, about seventy-five people from the audience joined me in one of the Dixon's galleries, where two Chagall paintings, *Dreamer* and *Bouquet of Flowers with Lovers*, are displayed. And from somewhere I found the energy to give another forty-five minute lecture on the two paintings.

It is a thrill to present a tribute to Chagall and Elvis, accompanied by the creative gift of a young composer. I feel Chagall and Elvis surrounding me and telling me I did very well indeed.

Chapter 14
A Gift to Chagall

How do you adequately acknowledge the remarkable way in which a friend has enriched your life? That question concerned me every time I lectured on Chagall. Yes, I was continuing to spread his message for world peace each time I made an appearance on his behalf. But what more could I do on a very personal level?

I had emphasized the significance of Chagall's belief in the integration of art and music by the commissioning of *Conversations*, which blended rock and roll with klezmer, the musical form rooted in ancient Jewish culture, and rich Russian symphonic-style melodies.

I knew that somehow music would have to be an essential part of any means by which I could express my gratitude for all that Chagall had given me. And I wanted to include Ralph in this expression of appreciation, for the gift of reconciliation that Chagall's stained glass windows at St. Stephan had brought to both of us.

Slowly, a thought took shape. We would celebrate our golden wedding anniversary on February 17, 2007. We didn't want to take a cruise or host a lavish dinner party for many friends and family members. In fact, when I first broached the subject with Ralph, he responded, "Something simple, like going to a movie and then going out for coffee."

Both of us are lovers of classical music, and we were season ticket holders for the half dozen concerts each year given by the North Carolina Symphony in our area. On one of those occasions, we listened with delight to an original tone poem, *Sketches of Pinehurst*, composed by Terry Mizesko, a member of the orchestra.

As we recalled that experience, we decided to mark the important occasion of our 50th wedding anniversary in a completely different way. Once again, we would commission a piece of music by Seth Weinstein. This time, the composition would be known as *The Chagall Suite* and would include different sections, each one dealing with a particular period of Chagall's life or aspect of his work.

Seth, recently represented on the New York stage as the composer of a critically acclaimed Off-Broadway musical comedy, *How to Save the*

91

World' and Find Love in 90 Minutes, was fascinated with the concept of returning to a more serious vein of composing, especially one that would allow him to musically express the great artistry of Marc Chagall. "It would be a refreshing break from my theatrical work," he remarked.

Together we decided on the various segments of the piece – eight in all. The titles of the sections are: *Vitebsk; The Bible; The Circus; Lovers and Flowers; The Prince of Peace, Jesus and the Prophet of Peace, Isaiah; Paris; Nature;* and *Angels.*

To help begin the creative process, I provided Seth with a folder for each section. These folders contained representative examples of Chagall's art work, as well as excerpts of Chagall's writings on the subjects. I also added the Chuck Olin videos and several books from my collection with reproductions of Chagall's masterpieces.

Weinstein related later: "After I became familiar with Chagall's work, little ideas started forming in my head, and a lot of the composition took place in bed at night, or during one of my therapeutic walks around New York City over the course of the next several months.

The themes of the eight short sections are interconnected to some extent. The opening section depicts the small town in Russia that was Chagall's birthplace. When he painted scenes from his hometown, there is an essence of the daily life and the Jewish ritual of evening prayer that I tried to incorporate in the music."

In the section dealing with peace, Weinstein used well-rounded chordal structures, as well as some more plaintive themes. He found geometry in Chagall's work that is echoed by the natural geometry in music. And he musically spelled out Chagall's name in more than one section.

Weinstein explained, "I translated the letters in his name to notes on the scale, substituting 'b' for 'h', which was done in old German musical literature, and using the double 'l' as the numeral 11. This gave me the notes 'c,' 'b,' 'a,' 'g,' 'a,' and then the eleventh note above the 'c'."

Chagall's love for the Bible and his belief that it was the greatest book ever written is explored in a special section devoted to Biblical themes. The section on the Circus is a reflection of Chagall's lifelong fascination of this performance art. The section on Paris gave Weinstein the greatest challenge. He further commented, "since there are so many familiar musical scores about Paris, and I didn't want to duplicate any of the typical sounds."

The obvious date for the world premiere of *The Chagall Suite* was the day of our golden wedding anniversary, and the beautiful setting for the momentous occasion was the Great Room of the Weymouth Center for the Arts and Humanities, once the lovely southern home of the late James and Katherine Boyd. Weymouth has become the cultural centerpiece of Moore County, and Ralph has served on its music committee for many of years.

Now that we had the particulars sorted out, I started to plan the invitation. I wanted it, of course, to be grand – a reproduction of a Chagall image. But, which one? I considered *The Bridal Procession* and *Lovers in the Bouquet of Roses*. Then I came across a Chagall book that I hadn't looked at in years. Ralph had had a special bookcase made for all my books on Chagall, and in going through and reorganizing the material, I found *Chagall by Chagall*, published by Harry Abrams & Company.

As I opened the book, I rediscovered on the inside flyleaf an original drawing that Chagall had done for Ralph's 53rd birthday. I was stunned, as I had totally forgotten about this drawing, and the more I looked at it, the more I realized it would be the perfect cover for our 50th wedding anniversary invitation.

All these years, people had asked me if I had an original piece of Chagall art and I had always said no completely overlooking this drawing that he had done in black ink and red and green crayon. It is so Chagall, so lovely, so meaningful.

The drawing is of a couple, surely Ralph and me, in addition to some trees with graceful black-inked limbs and circular branches of green and red, reaching toward the sky. On the bottom left-hand border, there is a little chicken, which is so often found in Chagall's lithographs and paintings, and of course Chagall's signature with a message - "Pour Ralph, Bon Anniversaire 15/1/1981."

I was struck with happiness and said a silent thank you to the Chagall angel who had led me to open this book which had been ignored for more than twenty-five years. I showed Ralph the two reproductions I had previously chosen and the original drawing and asked him to pick the one he wanted to use on the invitation. Without hesitation, he pointed to the drawing.

About this time, I found a copy of a note I wrote to Chagall's granddaughter, Bella. "Planning for the anniversary is more exciting than getting married."

From Chagall, I had learned many things. Among them were the importance of the quality of the paper and the accurate reproduction of colors. It took several months before we arrived at the precise combination of the two elements, which occurred before we could decide on the selection of the proper size of the invitation, the font to be used, the envelopes, the return envelopes, and even the right postage stamp.

The end result was just as Chagall would have wanted it. Many of our guests, when responding to the invitation, told us that they were going to have it framed and hung as a genuine piece of Chagall's art work. It was a confirmation of our desire to share Chagall with our friends and family. The invitation was also certainly in tune with the commissioned piano piece.

The day before the premiere performance I sat enthralled, listening as Seth rehearsed. I closed my eyes and there before me, as he played, was painting after painting and image after image. He had indeed captured the heart and spirit of Chagall through music.

We had made arrangements for the world premiere to be a two day event. The first performance was on Saturday evening, a private affair for special guests, family and people who had become close friends through the years.

The Saturday night celebration included a cocktail buffet reception held before the concert. I wore a stunning hand painted sheer blouse with pink and rose-colored flowers over a sleeveless black velvet sheath, and Ralph, looking charming in a new suit, as we greeted the guests. In contrast to the meaningful Chagall quotes that were included in the elegant program for the affair, I gave a little introductory speech with humorous overtones, such as my mother's comment, "What do you mean you don't want to marry Ralph Jacobson? You are going to marry him whether you like it or not!" With Ralph contributing some interrupting remarks in his own witty style, we received huge laughs.

Then on Sunday afternoon, there was a second performance, open to the public. After the concert, the Women of Weymouth produced and prepared a Russian tea, in honor of Chagall. Lots of chocolates and candies were served to honor the master.

On both Saturday night and Sunday afternoon, Seth began the concert by playing *Conversations*. He prefaced his performance of *The Chagall Suite* with a masterful presentation of Beethoven's *Waldstein Piano Sonata #21 in C* and the *Mozart Piano Sonata #19 in D*.

Dr. Joseph Aceves, a retired professor and ardent music lover who has written music reviews for *The Pilot*, a local publication, called *The Chagall Suite*, "A Joy."

In his commentary on the world premiere, Dr. Aceves wrote, "Musically, *The Chagall Suite* is really impossible to categorize. It includes elements of just about every Western musical form one can imagine – romanticism, impressionism, Jewish folk music and jazz. One is reminded of the show music of Andrew Lloyd Webber that utilizes a wide variety of musical styles. Weinstein does somewhat the same thing, only in my judgment, does it better. Chagall is famous for his use of colors, and Weinstein brings out the colors by a variety of sound changes and styles.

Chagall's message of love as universal, the composer exhibits universality through various musical styles and devices. It is extraordinarily wonderful music – it must be heard again and by more people. Properly orchestrated, it would be a valuable contribution to symphonic music."

Dr. Aceves complimented us by noting that we had given music lovers a gift of love and joy expressed through the music of a gifted young composer, Seth Weinstein. "Thanks to the Jacobsons, we received Chagall's message lovingly and eloquently expressed in sound."

Our golden wedding anniversary tribute to Chagall was the extraordinary result of a thirty-two year rapport with this 20th century icon. It was a splendid climax to the decades of close friendship, with still more Chagallian moments to come.

In the following months, I immersed myself in an attempt to bring *The Chagall Suite* to a larger audience. I had conversations with the North Carolina Symphony about a future orchestration, and in the meantime successfully arranged Seth Weinstein to play the composition at several concerts – both in the United States and Germany in 2008. A compact disc has been produced and is currently available of Seth Weinstein's two original pieces of music played at the 50th Wedding Anniversary concerts – *Conversations* and *The Chagall Suite*. It may be ordered online by accessing http://cdbaby.com/cd/sethweinstein or by calling 1-800-289-6923. And I naturally have continued with my series of lectures.

I have never wanted to keep Chagall to myself. I have shared him with others through my lectures, and now through these two wonderful pieces of music.

The response that I most often hear from my lecture audiences is that they love the personal stories I tell about Chagall. It is a reaction that eclipses anything else that I may include about the meaning of a painting, or a stained glass window. My audiences range from people who know very little about art or Chagall to people who are art collectors, art historians and curators and are knowledgeable about art history and have studied Chagall's paintings at length.

I estimate that I have been able to connect with well over ten thousand people through my lectures. However, in keeping with my desire to share my friendship with the artist Chagall, writing this book has been the best way I have to reach out and relate my own experiences with Chagall, the person.

The simple fact is that I have thought about writing this book for several years. I have been encouraged to do so by individuals and by other authors and scholars of Chagall that I have come to know and respect. So by sharing Chagall, I can continue my life's work. With my dear friend, Chagall, I have joined forces, contributing to world peace by carrying on his message of hope, peace, reconciliation and love

Chagall would always express his approval or disapproval in one of two unspoken ways. His disapproval of a project was marked by a sideways forceful flick of his right hand with a pointed finger going downward from left to right. If his final judgment was negative, a painting or lithograph or tapestry would be scrapped entirely and a new effort made to achieve his highest standards. On the other hand, he would signify his approval by a slow nodding of his head.

I hope and pray that Chagall has given that critical nod to this book.

May the memory of Marc Chagall be a blessing forever.

The above photograph was taken during The Jacobsons 50th wedding anniversary trip to Alaska and Vancouver, British Columbia.
August 2007

Photo courtesy of Jane H. Buchanan

Chapter 1: Goldie Dellsy, President of the Chicago Chapter of
Hadassah presenting Marc Chagall with a plaque designating him
as a Hadassah Associate.

Photo courtesy of Morris (Moe) Spector

Chapter 5: Chagall and Vivian Jacobson reviewing the
dedication speech for the harpsichord. January 4, 1981

Photo courtesy of Elizabeth Ragan

Chapter 5: The famous Harpsichord showing Chagall's painting of
Rebecca and Isaac on the inside cover of the instrument. January 4, 1981.

Photo courtesy of Musée National Message Biblique Marc Chagall

Chapter 6: Stained glass window depicting the Virgin Mary and the Child
at the St. Stephan Church, Mainz, Germany.

Photo courtesy of Kunstverlag Maria Laach

Chapter 9: The paint brushes of Marc Chagall

Photo courtesy of Chuck Olin

Chapters 10 and 11: *Job* tapestry at the
Rehabilitation Institute of Chicago. Dedicated June 20, 1986

Chapter 14: This Chagall original drawing with an inscription by the artist on the title page of the book *Chagall by Chagall* was given to Ralph Jacobson for his birthday in 1981. It was later used as the cover for our 50th wedding anniversary invitation.

Acknowledgements

The idea for this book grew out of a conversation that I had with Professor Benjamin Harshav of Yale University in February 2004. He had recently published a monumental book on Chagall entitled *Marc Chagall and His Times: A Documentary Narrative.* I had traveled to New Haven to meet with him and discuss the book.

On that winter day, Professor Harshav and I shared one story after another about Chagall. All of a sudden he turned to me and said, "You should write a book about Chagall. Everyone writes about his artwork, but nobody today writes about the personality of Chagall. Your book would help all kinds of students and authors of Chagall to understand the artist through his personal characteristics."

The outline and draft of some of the chapters were written at the Weymouth Center for the Arts and Humanities in Southern Pines, North Carolina. My thanks to this wonderful cultural center and the chairman of the writer in residence program, Cos Barnes. The quiet, the peace and the beauty of Weymouth gave me the inspiration and motivation needed to begin the task of transferring into the written word, the memories of a very special friendship with a remarkable artist and poet.

The majority of the research work came from my personal Chagall library of over 300 books, catalogues, magazines, articles, private correspondence, and photos. But the project also necessitated documentation and research of materials beyond those that I had in my possession. I would like to thank the Ryerson Library of the Art Institute of Chicago and the Sandhills Community College Library of Pinehurst, North Carolina, for making available their special librarians who provided invaluable information. Their patience with me was unbelievable.

This book also would not have been possible without the great friendship and interest of Chagall's two granddaughters, Bella Meyer of New York and Meret Meyer of Paris.

To Mary Elle Hunter, a real Chagall angel, who helped to organize and edit this book, I say a very large thank you for her perseverance and understanding, as we sorted through 18 boxes of material which had to be reviewed to bring this book to fruition.

To John Pecaric, a true lover of books, for his superb knowledge of the publishing industry and sharing that detailed knowledge with me.

I extend my personal thanks to my advisor, Ted Dawes, of SCORE, Counselors to America's Small Business, who volunteered to share his wealth of knowledge in the fields of publishing and marketing.

I also want to express exceptional thanks to Kim Gilley of Village Printers, Pinehurst, North Carolina, whose high standards, computer and graphic skills helped produced this book that measures up to the standards of which the artist Marc Chagall himself certainly would have approved. To Gayle Parker, my deepest gratitude for her brilliant understanding of the English language and its use. A gracious thank you to my secretary, Patty Lunday, and to Ed Gideon, business coach, who urged me to once again present the lecture, "Elvis and Chagall."

Finally, thank you to my wonderful and incredible husband Ralph, to whom I dedicate this book, for his understanding and devotion to the project of my *SHARING CHAGALL: A MEMOIR*.

Vivian R. Jacobson
June 2016
Pinehurst, North Carolina

APPENDIX

This appendix is to further the reader's interest in the artist Marc Chagall. While I have written about the personality and character of Chagall, the appendix speaks about his art. It is a special bibliography and a one-of-a-kind resource.

The listings are based on visits to exhibitions and research for my lectures. Each item listed is of unique quality and it is with that quality that I want to share with the reader in my book SHARING CHAGALL: A MEMOIR

    I. My Lectures on Chagall   page 108
   II. Books-Introduction page 111
      Books for Adults page 111
      Books for Children   page 120
  III. Catalogues-Introduction   page 123
      Museum Exhibitions   page 124
      Art Galleries   page 129
  IV. Chagall Museums and Additional Information   page 130
   V. Museum Listings Displaying Chagall Artworks Worldwide page 132
  VI. Libraries for Research   page 133
 VII. Magazine Articles   page 135
VIII. DVDs and Videos   page 137
  IX. Music CDs   page 138
   X. Postcard Books   page 140
  XI. Internet Sites – Where to Buy Books New and Old,
      Catalogues, DVDs, CDs, Videos, Posters and Visuals   page 141
 XII. Posters and Photos   page 142
XIII. The Discovered and Undiscovered Chagall   page 142
XIV. The Fifteen Stained Glass Windows of Chagall
      Listed by Country and in Chronological Order   page 144
 XV. Speeches   page 146
      Welcoming Marc Chagall to Our Home in Chicago
      Harpsichord Dedication
      Rehabilitation Institute of Chicago
      The 25th Anniversary Memorial of the Passing of Marc Chagall
XVI. Members of the Rehabilitation Institute of Chicago,
      Friends of the Chagall Tapestry Committee   page 150
XVII. Bibliography   page 151

My Lectures on Chagall

*Chagall and The Bible

From his earliest years in Vitebsk, Belarus, Chagall was fascinated by the Bible. The lecture covers twelve major paintings from *Genesis* and *Exodus*, and the *Song of Songs* paintings inspired by his second wife, Vava Chagall on permanent display at the Chagall Biblical Message Museum in France, as well as the stained glass windows of *The Creation of the Earth*, the famous harpsichord painting of Rebecca and Isaac, the mosaic of the prophet Elijah and a tapestry.

Chagall in Israel: Exploring Chagall's Artistic and Spiritual Legacy

Although some of Chagall's biographers have thought his relationship to Israel was linked to a commission illustrating the Bible, actually his first trip to Palestine in 1931 heightened his enduring bond with his Hasidic Jewish heritage. He maintained close ties with artists, art historians, politicians, writers and businessmen, in Israel extending the depth of his involvement with each of his seven visits. This lecture examines these artistic pilgrimages which serve as an introduction to his paintings and other artwork that he donated to the Israel Museum in Jerusalem and the Tel Aviv Museum. In addition a sampling of sketches, drawings and other works found in both private and public collections is included in the lecture.

Chagall and the Printed Word

An in-depth examination of letters, books, catalogues, invitations, postcards, newspapers, and magazine articles from the Jacobson private collection.

Chagall and Chicago

A lecture, accompanied by images and two short documentary films, devoted to the three major Chagall works done for the city of Chicago -- a mosaic, *The Four Seasons*, at the former First National Bank of Chicago Plaza, the *America Windows*, and the *Job* tapestry at the Rehabilitation Institute of Chicago. Also included in the discussion are the two famous Chagall paintings on display at the Art Institute of Chicago – the *White Crucifixion* and *The Praying Jew*.

The Color of Love

A special presentation for children of all ages, using images and telling stories of Chagall from his childhood in Russia to his life in France. Featured as part of the lecture are 100 postcards of Chagall's paintings, which children can handle, as well as a question and answer segment.

My Favorite Top 10 Artworks of Marc Chagall

A visual presentation and lecture of my 10 favorite Chagall artworks and why they are important to me and to the world.

*The Chagall Harpsichord

A lecture and image presentation on the replica of an 18th century French Blanchet harpsichord located at the Chagall Biblical Message Museum. A gift by the American Friends of the Museum, the harpsichord's inside cover contains a Chagall painting of the love story of Rebecca and Isaac.

*The Jerusalem Windows: The Twelve Tribes of Israel

Among Chagall's crowning achievements in the media of stained glass are the twelve windows he designed for the Hadassah-Hebrew University Medical Center in Jerusalem in 1959-61, with each of the windows representing a tribe of Israel. Chagall filled them with a dazzling assembly of animal forms, heavenly bodies and other elements symbolic of each tribe.

*The Windows of Reconciliation: The St. Stephan Church, Mainz, Germany

This lecture on the windows was first suggested by the parish priest, Klaus Mayer. The windows were designed by Chagall for the apse of the church in 1973 as a sign of hope, peace, reconciliation and love for France and Germany, and for Christians and Jews. Use of images illustrates each section of the windows. The lecture contains a detailed analysis of the artwork as it coincides with Chagall's passion for the Bible.

*The Christ Configuration in the Artworks of Chagall

A visual show presentation on the Christ configuration of the crucifixion and resurrection as interpreted by Marc Chagall in stained glass windows and paintings. For Chagall, Christ was the symbol of the ultimate suffering of all mankind.

Chagall and the Women in His Life

A discussion of the part the women in Chagall's life played in his becoming one of the greatest artists of the 20th century; his grandmother, mother, six sisters, his two wives, Bella Rosenfield and Vava Brodsky, his companion Virginia Haggard, his daughter Ida and granddaughters, Bella Meyer and Meret Meyer. The lecture includes images of paintings influenced by each woman, and also features the writings of Bella and Marc Chagall.

The Literary Chagall
Hope, Peace, Reconciliation and Love: The Messages of Marc Chagall in His Art and Literature.

The lecture is an overview of the artist's love of writing poetry and prose. Few people know that Chagall had a pronounced literary ability equal to that of his art. Included is an introduction to his poetry and prose, and a visual presentation showing the artworks that inspired his writings.

Elvis and Chagall

What do a famous artist and the King of Rock and Roll have in common? A fascinating comparison of two 20th century icons that demonstrates how their great passion for their art gave them a commonality -- their deep respect for religion, their total control of their art which elevated viewers and listeners to an advanced level, and their need for women in their lives for inspiration and to sustain their sense of creativity. The lecture uses a multi-media approach with the presentation of images of paintings by Chagall offered to a recorded background of Presley's music.

Flowers by Chagall

"Art is the increasing effort to compete with the beauty of flowers - and never succeeding." Such were the words of Marc Chagall. A passion for nature in the form of flowers, trees, birds and animals fill the artworks of Chagall. His love of flowers and his interpretation of these wonders of nature are consistently found in every form of his magnificent creations. This lecture will bring this concept of how Chagall brought his love of flowers to his numerous works of art. Flowers were consistently present in his studio to give him inspiration and for making his artistic ideas become reality.

*Lecture contains selected readings from relevant Biblical passages.
For lecture presentations contact ravi@pinehurst.net.

Books – Introduction

There are thousands of books on Chagall. In this section, I have included books which I feel can help the reader to do his/her own follow-up research and further study of Chagall. Here are some of my favorites, all with great text and excellent reproductions. I hope you will share my enthusiasm.

Note: One of the most remarkable websites for locating books and catalogues on Chagall is **www.worldcat.org/identities/lccn-n79-43105.**

This site lists 4,373 works on Chagall in 9,131 publications in 22 languages in 100,904 library holdings! This site also provides a full description of books, catalogues, etc., and where to buy them. Most important is that when you find the title, click, type in your zip code and VOILA! There will be a list of libraries where you can find the book with the distance given from the library to your home.

There is also a unique cross-reference by years from 1900 to 2016. Click on to a year in which you are especially interested, and you will find publications written during that year about Marc Chagall, including those published posthumously.

Consequently, to find the nearest library that has a book or catalogue listed in this appendix and bibliography. All you have to do is access the website, then click in the year, the title of the book or catalogue, enter your zip code, and the publication will be shown at the closest library for your area. You may also need to access the Internet for books and catalogues that are out of print.

Books for Adults

Chagall – Keramik

Sylvie Forestier – Meret Meyer
Hirmer Verlag, München, Germany
1990
German
181 pages (including catalogue information)
ISBN 3-7774-53890-0

If a catalogue, museum catalogue or a book has the names of the authors Meret Meyer or Bella Meyer, the granddaughters of Marc Chagall, then you can be sure of the authenticity of the written word, superb photographic reproductions, and detailed informative bibliography.

This exquisite book, written in German, accurately describes Chagall's adventure into the field of ceramics from 1949 – 1972. If you have any interest in pottery or ceramics this book is for you.

Plates, pitchers, vases, tiles, cups and saucers all designed and created with fabulous colors hand painted by the master are included. Who but Chagall could make the handle of a water pitcher into the form of a very sensuous woman?

Marc Chagall and His Times: A Documentary Narrative

Benjamin Harshav

Stanford University Press, Stanford, California

2004

English

1026 pages

ISBN 0-407-4214-6

Benjamin Harshav is the Jacob and Hilda Blaustein Professor of Hebrew and Comparative Literature at Yale University. Every one of his books on Chagall is a gem.

This book presents a new and definitive biography of the artist through hundreds of private letters and documents that were written by Chagall, his friends, family and art associates. The material is translated from Russian, Yiddish, French and English by Benjamin Harshav and his wife Barbara Harshav. The book has superb photos and drawings of Chagall's artwork. The interaction between Chagall and the people in his life and all of the documents are fascinating. In my opinion the correspondence and the documents regarding the personal life and the artistic life of Chagall and the placement of these documents in the book, all 1026 pages, are worth every penny of the cost. Every page is blessed with manuscripts that are never found in other books. Harshav has the ability to do never-ending research, translation and has an impeccable presentation.

Marc Chagall on Art and Culture

Edited by Benjamin Harshav

Stanford University Press, Stanford, California

2003

English

225 pages

ISBN 0-8047-4631-4

This book is published in English and translated from French, Russian, Yiddish and Hebrew by Benjamin and Barbara Harshav. Documents, interviews and the poetry and prose of Marc Chagall are included in this book. The reader will acquire a feel for the life of the artist between the early 1920s and 1985. The first book on Marc Chagall was written in 1918 by A. Efros and Ya. Tugendhold and published by Helicon and is included in this volume.

Marc Chagall and the Lost Jewish World

The Nature of Chagall's Art and Iconography

Benjamin Harshav

Rizzoli, New York, New York

1996

English

256 pages

ISBN 0-8478-2802-6

A beautiful book with numerous and attractive reproductions of Chagall's artwork. This book is filled with information on the details of Chagall's early life in Vitebsk, Belarus and the Hasidic movement of the Jews in the 18th and 19th century. Very often I receive phone calls or e-mails from lecturers who want to know more about Chagall's early life. This is the book I recommend for further research. Rizzoli has done an outstanding job of clear and concise reproductions of Chagall's artwork.

Marc Chagall: Painting as Poetry

Ingo F. Walther and Rainer Metzger

Taschen, Cologne, Germany

2006

English

95 pages

ISBN 3-8228-5990-7

This is an inexpensive paperback to purchase for your friends and family. The book contains quotes by Chagall, which can be interpreted as explanations of his paintings. Also included in the book are poetry and quotations by poets who wrote about Chagall. I have given this book to young people for their Bar or Bat Mitzvah and birthday presents and to adults for wedding gifts and special events in their lives, always with the inscription "with Chagallian wishes." The book has a superb chronology with black and white photos of the artist and his family.

Marc Chagall

Jacob Baal -Teshuva

Taschen, Cologne, Germany

1998

English

279 pages

ISBN 3-8228-5994-X

The author, Jacob Baal-Teshuva, has written a large book with great reproductions of Chagall's paintings and also includes tapestries, mosaics, stained glass, sculptures and ceramics. Each chapter begins with a quote from Chagall regarding the subject matter. The book is dedicated in memory of Ida Chagall (1916-1994), the artist's daughter who was devoted to her father. After the hardback was no longer published, Taschen published a very lovely edition in paperback with the cover of a sweet Chagall angel carrying a brightly lit menorah. Baal-Teshuva has written other books on Chagall, all of them most informative with a great deal of research.

Marc Chagall: The Lithographs

The Collection of Charles Sorlier

A Catalogue Raisonne

D.A.P. New York, New York

1998

English, French and German

413 pages

ISBN 1-891024-07-8 (English edition)

For the money, this is the best book ever on the lithographs of the artist Marc Chagall. There are 1050 depicted in this magnificent volume. The lithographs were produced by Charles Sorlier, who was a friend and the lithographer of Chagall. There is a brief history about the Fernand Meurlot workshop in Paris, an essay by Hans Kinkel, and interviews with Henri Deschamp, Charles Marq and Christofer Conrad.

Three pages are devoted to the technique of lithography based on the observations and interpretations of the artist. Numerous illustrations include those from the Bible, the circus, lovers, and scenes of Paris. The lithographs begin in the year 1922 and continue on to the time of Chagall's death in 1985. A wonderful, wonderful, unbelievable non-stop book representing the energy of the artist. A great wedding present! One that the bride and groom will cherish forever.

Burning Lights

Bella Chagall and illustrated by Marc Chagall

Biblio Press, New York

1996

English

268 pages

ISBN 0-930395-26-3

I love this little book. The translation is from the Yiddish by Norbert Guterman, with an introduction by Judith Baskin. This autobiography of Bella, Chagall's first wife, tells about her life and love for Chagall from the time they first met to the time of her death in September of 1944. This book exudes their incredible and passionate relationship as husband and wife through wonderful short stories of the life they had in Vitebsk. With the illustrations it is a social history of the Hasidic Jewish life that surrounded them in the late 19th century. There is also a glossary of Hebrew and Yiddish words.

Chagall

Monica Bohm-Duchen

Phaidon Press Limited, London, England

English

1998

330 pages

ISBN: 0714831603

This dynamite biography of Chagall by Monica Bohm-Duchen is superb in every way. The layout of the book is easy to read, to take notes and/ or add comments. It has wide margins, good spacing between the sentences, typeset in Strayhorn, and printed in Italy.

This scholarly book has amazing photos of family and friends, and great reproductions of Chagall artworks and other artists in reference to Chagall. The bonus of this book is the glossary of art terminology, and brief biographies of artists who were associated with Chagall. Additionally, there are key dates in the life of Chagall and their relationship to world events. A map of Europe with borders at the end of the 20th century is also included. I love this book, and you will too!

Marc Chagall: My Life

Marc Chagall

The Orion Press, New York, New York

English

1960

175 pages

Library of Congress Number 60-83-61

This autobiography was translated by Elisabeth Abbott and has 23 sweet and warm illustrations by the author. The literary ability of Chagall as shown in this book comes through as a shining star. The book was written when Chagall was 35 years old. One can really absorb the spirit of his birthplace, Vitebsk, and for his family and friends. The joy of the world of his Jewish background is examined with perfect words. I have read this book three times, and I continue to admire the fact that he wrote this book at an early age and that he lived to 97. All of his artwork, one way or another, is autobiographical.

Books by Klaus Mayer: St. Stephan Church, Mainz, Germany
The God of the Fathers

Volume 1, Center Window

Echter Publishing House, Wurzburg, Germany

1993

English

54 pages

ISBN 3-429-01419-0

I Have Set My Bow in the Clouds

Volume 2, The Flanking Centre Windows

Echter Publishing House, Wurtzburg, Germany

1995

English

82 pages

ISBN 3-429-01644-4

Lord, My God, How Great You Are!

Volume 3, The Flanking Windows

Echter Publishing House, Wurzburg, Germany

1995

English

75 pages

ISBN 3-429-01684-3

Heaven and the Highest Heavens Cannot Contain You

Volume 4, The Windows in the Transept

Echter Publishing House, Wurtzburg, Germany

1996

English

62 pages

ISBN 3-429-01751-3

All four of these volumes are absolutely gorgeous in their reproductions of the Chagall windows at the St. Stephan Church, Mainz, Germany. The Maria Lach photography is responsible for staying so true to the colors of Marc Chagall. The grisaille work done in an iron oxide pigment brings out the colors of Chagall like a woman wearing mascara. The famous acid wash is present in each section of the window panes.

The writing of Father Klaus Mayer is so spiritual that you do not have to read the Old Testament for inspiration, just read these four volumes. They are certainly filled with the love and attention that Chagall would have given personally to these windows of reconciliation.

My Life with Chagall: Seven Years of Plenty with the Master as Told by the Woman Who Shared Them

Virginia Haggard

Donald Fine, Inc., New York, New York

1986

English

190 pages

ISBN 0-917657-X

Virginia Haggard met Chagall in 1945 when Chagall was 58 years old and she was 31. She had become Chagall's companion within a year of the death of his beloved Bella. Together they had a son, David. The book reveals their life in America and France from the period of 1945-1952. The book includes a wonderful correspondence between her and Chagall and photos. Make this book a definite read.

Marc Chagall

Franz Meyer

Harry N. Abrams, Inc., New York, New York

1963 - 1964

English

783 pages

ISBN 9109-0055-6

This definitive volume was the first large-scale book on Chagall published in the United States. Franz Meyer, the author, was the son-in-law of Chagall and an art historian. The book is filled with reproductions and explanations of his paintings. The author catalogued all of Chagall's paintings from 1906-1964. There are also photos of ceramics, sculptures and stained glass windows and other Chagall artworks. Brilliant, brilliant, brilliant! The magical realism of Chagall shines through every page. There are 1,250 illustrations and 53 tipped in color plates. This book can usually be found in a high quality second hand bookstore. A must have for the Chagall student and scholar.

Chagall

Andrew Kagan

Abbeville Press, New York, New York

1989

English

128 pages

ISBN 089659-935-3

This book is part of the Modern Masters Series of the publishing house Abbeville Press. Kagan has written a good biography with some black and white reproductions, as well as those in color. There is a fine photo of the Chagall harpsichord at the Musée Chagall in Nice, France on page 99. The latter part of the book is filled with information for future research work on the part of the reader. It contains quotes of the artist.

The notes on the technique chapter are filled with information usually not available on other books. It includes the names of the people who worked with Chagall on the stained glass windows, tapestries and ceramics. This information is followed by a definitive chronology, a detailed list of exhibitions from 1914-1982, a list of public collections, and a selected bibliography. This book is one of my backup books for my lectures in terms of correct information. Kagan has given us his best.

Chagall by Chagall

Edited by Charles Sorlier

Harry N. Abrams, Inc., New York, New York

1979

French and English

263 pages

ISBN 08109-0758-5

This is the artist's autobiography, illustrated with beautiful artworks and his writings. Written in both English and French, this volume gives the reader a simultaneous view of his paintings and his written ideas. Chagall has organized this book according to the themes of his life and artwork. The back of the book has an excellent chronology plus great photographs of Chagall. The loveliest section begins on page 165 with the story of the ceiling of the Paris Opera House and Chagall's intimate friendship with André Malraux, the Minister of Culture during the administration of Charles de Gaulle.

Marc Chagall: Biblical Interpretations

Pierre Provoyeur

Alpine Fine Arts Collections, LTD, New York and London

1983

English and French

259 pages

ISBN 0933516-94-0

This large volume is devoted to the seventeen major paintings based on *Genesis* and *Exodus*; a cycle of five *Song of Songs*; stained glass windows relating the story of the creation of the earth and a mosaic based on the story of Prophet Elijah; all at the Biblical Message Museum of Marc Chagall, Nice, France. Other Biblical artworks and poetry of Chagall are also included in this volume. Superb reproductions and biblical quotations included. Included is a detailed history of Chagall's dream to have all his major biblical works housed in one museum.

Marc Chagall

Jonathan Wilson

Shocken Press and Nextbook. New York, New York

English

239 pages

ISBN 978-08052-4201-0

This biography of Chagall proves to the reader that we still have in to-day's world writers who really know how to write. He uses imaginative words of Chagall and his artwork like a painter painting a canvas. Only one reproduction which of course, is one of my very favorites: *The Lovers*, 1929 in the collection of the Tel Aviv museum in Israel.

The publisher has asked the reader to visit nextbook.org/Chagall for a virtual museum of Chagall images. There are some photos, but it is Wilson's writing that captures the exciting and extraordinary life of Marc Chagall.

Chagall

Sidney Alexander

G.P. Putnam's Sons, New York, New York

1978

English

526 pages

ISBN 399-11894-2

While this is a most detailed writing on the life of Marc Chagall, not one reproduction of Chagall's artwork is contained in the biography. However, the author has an eloquent and articulate way with words that "paints" the life of the artist. The author makes many comparative references to other artists and describes the relationship between Picasso and Chagall that you will find most interesting and not discussed in other books. The dust cover of the book is a portrait of Chagall by Yosuf Karsh of Ottawa, Canada. It is so wonderful that if you are a real Chagall fan, you can have the dust cover framed.

Books for Children

There are many books for children on Marc Chagall. Kids love the colors, the stories, animals and the floating, flowing figures. After all, he painted his childhood memories. Chagall loved children and children love Chagall. For holidays and birthdays, buy your child or grandchild an art book. Here are some suggestions!

Chagall Art Tattoos

Dover Publications, Inc., Minneola, New York, 1999

2 pages

ISBN 0-486-41668-2-4-2001

Chagall Art Stickers

Dover Publications, Inc., Minneola, New York, 1999

4 pages

ISBN 0-486-40598-2-16199

Both of these small books have a one-paragraph biography of Chagall and both have good reproductions. The children will love to "play" with Chagall.

Marc Chagall

Howard Greenfield

Harry N. Abrams, Energy Publications, New York, New York

1990

92 pages

ISBN 08109-3152-4

This superb book on Chagall is for the preteen years. It is part of the First Impressions services published by Harry N. Abrams. The author, Howard Greenfield, knew Marc Chagall and spent time with him talking about his life and work. The writing and reproductions are excellent.

I Am Marc Chagall

Bimba Landmann

Text and illustrations by Bimba Landmann

Text loosely inspired by My Life by Marc Chagall

Eerdmans Books for Young Readers, Grand Rapids, Michigan

2006

40 pages

ISBN 0-8028-5305-6

This book for young readers was based on Chagall's own writings. At the end there is a short biography on the life of Marc Chagall. Landman illustrated the book in her original three dimensional mixed media illustrations depicting the three main cities in Chagall's life: Vitebsk, Moscow, and Paris.

Marc Chagall: Painter of Dreams

Natalie S. Bober

Illustrated by Vera Rosenberry

The Jewish Publication Society, Philadelphia, Pennsylvania

1991

142 pages

ISBN 018276-0379-7

This book is written for children ages 8 to 12 and published as part of the Jewish Publication Society's Young Biography Series. Natalie Bober is an award-winning author on Abigail Adams. She also has published children's books on Robert Frost, Louise Nevelson and Thomas Jefferson, to name a few. This book is extremely well written with great illustrations by Vera Rosenberry.

Jewels for a Crown: The Story of the Chagall Windows

Miriam Freund

McGraw-Hill Book Company, Inc., New York, Toronto, London

1963

64 pages

Library of Congress No.63-19440

Dr. Miriam Freund, national president of Hadassah from 1956-1960, commissioned *The Jerusalem Windows, The Twelve Tribes of Israel* for the Hadassah Hospital synagogue. This book is unique because it has a complete, easy to read, easy to understand synopsis of how a Chagall window is made. The reproductions of the twelve windows are excellent. Miriam Freund has written a wonderful book for children.

Chagall For Children

Helene Lamarche

The Montreal Museum of Fine Arts, Montreal, Canada

1989

36 pages

This catalogue book for children was published on the occasion of the Marc Chagall exhibition from the collection of the Musée National d'art

Moderne, Centre George Pompidou. The book has good photos of Chagall and a great narrative to go with the selected paintings at the exhibition.

Marc Chagall

Written and illustrated by Mike Venezia

Children's Press: A division of Grolier Publishing, New York, New York

2000

32 pages

ISBN 0-516-21055-6

I love this little book as an introduction to Chagall for because the author
"believes the best way to introduce children to art and artists is through
fun." Since Chagall had a great sense of humor, the book represents an
extension of Chagall's personality. This book is wonderful, and I wish I had
it has a child.

Introduction to Catalogues

This section is about catalogues from Chagall museum exhibitions
and art galleries. At major art exhibitions there are books, catalogues and
other items for sale regarding the artist. Very often I am asked if a person
should buy a book or a catalogue about Chagall. My answer is buy the
catalogue.

I have found that catalogues are unique in their research and are a
product of a collaborative effort of the museum staff. When the budget is
created for an exhibition, the cost of the catalogue is included. The list of
sponsors for an exhibition can indicate the quantity of money spent for the
production of a catalogue; therefore, the quality can be determined.

Art exhibitions usually contain a number of artworks from private collections. They are catalogued along with well known artworks. Thus, often
the reader will find in catalogues, paintings and drawings that would or
could not be published in a book. I have found very good reproductions
and commentary in conjunction with the reproductions with detailed explanation of provenance.

In conclusion, museum exhibition catalogues on Chagall are a great buy.
Art gallery catalogues are usually free or can be purchased for a minimum
amount. In general, art galleries spend a great deal of money for repro-

ductions to entice a future buyer. Whether from museums or art galleries, catalogues on Chagall are a superb introduction to the artist and offer opportunities for research on Chagall.

Where to Find Catalogues

The best place to find old Chagall art gallery and museum exhibition catalogues is at a quality used bookstore. An example would be Moe's Bookstore in Berkeley, California. In Europe used bookstores abound with catalogues from exhibitions.

Museum Exhibition Catalogues

Marc Chagall and the Jewish Theater

Guggenheim Museum, New York, New York

Sept. 23, 1992-Jan. 17, 1993

English

207 pages

Chagall: Postmodernism and Fictional Worlds in Painting by Benjamin Harshav is included in this catalogue. The essay is worth the purchase. It also has wonderful notes and appendix sections.

The catalogue continues with essays about Chagall and the Yiddish theater, including an essay by M. Litvakov, *Five Years of the State Jewish Theater (1919-1924)*. The catalogue also includes the play *Agents: a Joke in One Act*, by Sholom Aleichem, and a section of essays, speeches, letters and poems by Marc Chagall.

Amazing reproductions of the theater murals really add to this catalogue. Take a few vitamin pills before you read this catalogue. It is powered by 100% of Chagall's energy.

Chagall: Love and the Stage

Royal Academy of Arts, London, England

July 2-October 4, 1998

English

103 pages

This catalogue gives a special importance to Chagall's initial theater design, beginning in St. Petersburg in 1910. His designs for set, costumes and masks are amazing. Here it is evident that Chagall's love of theater and the fate of his artwork under communism have remained strong, continuing on to The Metropolitan Opera in New York and The Paris Opera ceiling. The 'love' section of this catalogue presents some of his most treasured artwork with Bella, his first wife. Passion. Passion. Passion.

Marc Chagall: Les Années Russes 1907-1922

Musée d'Art Moderne, Paris, France

April 13-Sept. 17, 1995

French

228 pages

The Russian years were significant to the future of Chagall as an artist. The authors of this catalogue have dedicated themselves to a thorough investigation into these years with no less than fifteen detailed essays, and a monumental section of Chagall and the Jewish Theater.

The biography at the end of the book includes photos of artwork in the exhibition and also has a listing of exhibitions from 1906-1922. Fortunately, this catalogue comes with a children's edition as well. The whole project is superb.

Marc Chagall: 1907-1917

Museum of Fine Arts Berne, Berne, Switzerland

Jewish Museum in New York City, New York

Dec. 2, 1995-Feb. 28, 1996

German and English

205 pages

This catalogue, from an exhibition that was held in Berne, Switzerland, and at the Jewish Museum in New York, covers the artist's life and his artwork from 1907-1917. What a productive ten years Chagall gave to the world. Excellent reproductions and biography include the writings of Chagall. The New York exhibition catalogue came with an insert of painting information giving the following details as a synopsis: title of painting, year, medium used, size in inches and centimeters and from where the artwork was loaned.

This kind of exhibition and catalogue exhibits artwork from many private collections that are not available for viewing by the public. For this reason alone I made a special trip to see the exhibition. The catalogue is dedicated in memory of Ida Chagall, Chagall's daughter.

Chagall: Die Mythen der Bible

Albertina Museum, Vienna, Austria

Dec. 2, 2004-March 28, 2005

German

260 pages

I traveled to Vienna, Austria, to see this exhibition. It was an unbelievable experience. The uniqueness of this exhibition and catalogue was that all of the paintings were housed at the Albertina Museum while the Chagall Biblical Message Museum in Nice, France was being renovated. Seeing the large Bible paintings of Chagall in a new setting was a thrill beyond words.

The catalogue is exceptional as well, with great quality of paper, and excellent reproductions with comments about each painting. The authors of the catalogue have put their heart into it. But the most unusual aspects of the exhibition and catalogue are the displays of the initial drawings by Chagall for the Biblical Message Museum, with additional maquettes (cartoons) of the stained glass windows of the All Saints Church in Tudley, England, the tapestry in Jerusalem, Israel and the Cathedral in Chichester, England.

Superb biography and photos. Want to get your heart rate up without going on a treadmill? Turn to page 119!!

Marc Chagall: Oeuvres sur Papier

Musée National d'art Moderne-Centre Georges Pompidou, Paris, France

June 30 - October 8, 1984

French

240 pages

ISBN 2-85850-256-0

This extraordinary catalogue is devoted only to Chagall's works on paper. The catalogue is divided into sections based on what country Chagall was living in at the time. The catalogue is mostly of drawing reproductions in black and white with 51 in color. The text is by Pierre Provoyeur, who was the curator of the Chagall Biblical Message Museum in Nice, France. Detailed research and commentary molded for each drawing is included.

Chagall und Deutschland

The Jewish Museum of Frankfurt, Germany

Feb. 1-18 and May 1-Aug. 1, 2004

German

175 pages

If the Germans are known for one thing, it is their photographic precision for reproductions in catalogues for exhibitions, postcards and slides in documentation of artwork. This catalogue has outstanding reproductions of famous Chagall artworks and many from private collections.

Included are reproductions of the *St. Stephan Windows* in Mainz and the initial drawings for the Commedia dell 'arte, 1958, the mural for the Frankfurt Theater. An essay is also included about Chagall and the Holocaust with reproductions of the Christ configuration of the crucifixion and the resurrection.

I saw this exhibition four times in six days. The long lines of German citizens to view the exhibition and purchase the catalogue were a demonstration of the people's love for Chagall and to express their sorrow about the Holocaust.

Chagall

Kunsthaus Zurich, Switzerland

May 6-July 30, 1967

German

100 pages

This catalogue, forty years old, is a good example of a person walking into a used bookstore and finding a gem on Chagall. The outside cover has a beautiful bird in the shining sun of Paris and a woman . The inside cover has a great picture of Chagall.

Marc Chagall

The Montreal Museum of Fine Arts, Montreal, Canada

October 28, 1988 - Feb. 26, 1989

English

200 pages

This hard cover catalogue was created for the Chagall exhibition of artworks from the Musée National D'art Moderne Centre Georges Pompidou, Paris. The catalogue opens up with a 1947 joyful Chagall sitting in front of his masterpiece *I and the Village*. The last page of the catalogue has a wonderful photo of Chagall at Giverny in June 1963, at the home of Claude Monet.

The middle of the catalogue contains a special folder with the Christ configuration of the crucifixion and resurrection, all of these on quality paper with great reproductions. And of course the most important aspect of this catalogue are the brilliant essays by Jean Greir, *Chagall on the Poet*, and Edouard Roditi's *A Conversation with Chagall*.

Chagall from Russia to Paris

Drawings and Water Colors 1906-1967

Boca Raton Museum of Art, Boca Raton, Florida

January-February 2002

English

83 pages

I flew to Boca Raton, Florida, to see this unique exhibition. I could not pass up the opportunity to view this small exhibition from the David Mac-Neil collection. David MacNeil was the son of Marc Chagall and Virginia Haggard. Virginia was the companion/significant other of Marc Chagall between his first wife Bella and his second wife Valentina (Vava) Brodsky.

The exhibition was organized by II Centro Italian per le Arti e la Cultura in Rome from David's private collection. This "cache" of 70 sketches and small drawings is comprised of works that Chagall gave as gifts to his son David as he grew up. Also included in the exhibition catalogue are three sets of sketches: one for the choreographer Bronislava Nijinska's ballet, followed by the Bible and the story of Exodus.

If you love the small drawings by Chagall you will love this catalogue, especially *My House*, circa 1925. The little vegetable garden with the names of the vegetables written in Yiddish on tiny sign posts at the back yard of his home in Vitebsk is so special. It is priceless.

Art Gallery Catalogues

Marc Chagall: The Four Seasons

Pierre Matisse Gallery, New York, New York

May 1975

English and French

Pierre Matisse was the art agent for Chagall in the United States. The gallery was located on 57th Street in New York. This catalogue is filled with paintings that were on exhibit in the gallery. Included are small reproductions with large, wide borders, and the back of the catalogue has a listing of the paintings for sale. Included in the catalogue are reproductions of oil paintings from 1974-1975. Sometimes you do not need long essays in a catalogue – just the artwork speaks volumes.

Chagall

Galerie: Orangerie-Reinz

Köln, Germany

1982

German

96 pages

This catalogue was prepared by the gallery in honor of Chagall's 95th birthday. There are black and white reproductions of his drawings and color reproductions of the famous lithographs, no explanation of the artworks, just titles. The cover of the catalogue is worth the purchase.

Chagall-Vitebsk, St. Petersburg, Paris

Galerié Gérald Piltzer

March 5 to May 8, 1993

French

103 pages

This exhibition was in Paris, and I had the opportunity not only to view the works of Chagall but also those of Yehuda Pen, Chagall's first art teacher in Vitebsk. This is a rare catalogue, as it includes the artwork of both artists. The Yehuda Pen paintings were on loan from the Musée des Beaux – Arts de Vitebsk.

Together Chagall and Pen give us a synopsis of the social, political and economic themes of Vitebsk, Belarus in the late 19th century. I love this catalogue as it gave me a pictorial heritage of the lives of my grandparents and great grandparents in Lodz, Poland and Kishniev, Russia.

Marc Chagall

Timothy Yarger: Fine Arts, Beverly Hills, California

1999

English

76 pages

The Yarger gallery has produced a superb catalogue with an introduction by Timothy Yarger. Yarger lists the emotions that Chagall experienced to create his art. Included are great quotes by Chagall, a wonderful photo, paintings and lithographs and the hand colored etchings for *The Fables of Fontaine*. This catalogue is great bedside reading!

Chagall Museums

Check the Internet for exhibitions, days and hours open to the public, addresses and phone numbers.

Musée Marc Chagall

Avenue du Dr. Menard

06000 Nice, France

This museum is one of a kind. It is not only a museum, but also a place for one to feel his or her own spirituality. (The museum was formerly known as the Museé National Message Biblique Marc Chagall. See Chapter Four for a full description.)

Marc Chagall Museum, Vitebsk

Pokrovskaia Street, 29

2, Putna Street,

Vitebsk, Belarus

Chagall's renovated boyhood home on Pokrovskaya Street and the Marc Chagall Art Center on Putna Street created in 1992 represent outstanding reminders of the artist's early years. At the home you can experience a feeling for Hasidic Jewish life in the early 20th century because of the collection of articles of family life. You are able to view copies of archived documents, and works of Chagall pertaining to the family's life in Vitebsk. At the entrance of this street is a marvelous large sculpture of Chagall.

The Art Center exhibits a wide variety of Chagall's graphic works, including xylographs, lithographs, etchings, and aquatints. Among the museum's collections is a series of illustrations to Nicolai Gogol's poem *Dead Souls*, and color lithographs on the theme of the Bible, *The Twelve Tribes of Israel* and other works of Chagall.

Additional Information

For further inquiry and general information regarding exhibitions, authentication of Chagall artworks and the Ida Chagall Archives, contact:

> Comité Chagall
> Ida Chagall Archives
> 35 Quai de l'horloge
> 75001, Paris, France

For rights to reproduce a Chagall artwork or Chagall signature, contact:

> Janet Hicks, Director
> Artists Rights Society
> 536 Broadway
> 5th Floor
> New York, New York 10012
> 212-420-9160

Museum and Public Space Listings
Displaying Chagall Artworks Worldwide
as documented by
Andrew Kagan: Chagall – Modern Masters Series,
Abbeville Press, New York, New York 1990
Public Collections According to Cities and Countries

Amsterdam, The Netherlands, Stedlijk Museum.

Basel, Switzerland, Offentiche Kunstsammlung, Kunstmuseum Basel.

Berne, Switzerland, Kunstmuseum Berne.

Buffalo, New York, Albright-Knox Art Gallery.

Chicago, Illinois, Art Institute of Chicago.

Chicago, Illinois, First National Bank of Chicago.

Chichester, England, Chichester Cathedral.

Cologne, West Germany, Wallraf-Richartz-Museum.

Dusseldorf, West Germany, Kunstsammlung Nordrhein-Westfalen.

Eindhoven, The Netherlands, Stedelijk van Abbemuseum.

Florence, Italy, Galleria degli Uffizi.

Frankfurt, West Germany, Frankfurt Theater.

Göteborg, Sweden, Göteborgs Konstmuseum.

Hamburg, West Germany, Hamburger Kunsthalle.

Helsinki, Finland, Art Museum of the Ateneum.

Jerusalem, Israel, Bezalel National Art Museum.

Jerusalem, Israel, Israel Museum.

Jerusalem, Israel, Knesset.

Jerusalem, Israel, Synagogue of the Medical Center,
    Hadassah-Hebrew University.

Leningrad, Soviet Union, Ministry of Culture.

Leningrad, Soviet Union, State Russian Museum.

London, England, Tate Gallery.

Los Angeles, California, Los Angeles County Museum of Art.

Lugano, Switzerland, Thyssen-Bornemisza Collection.

Mainz, West Germany, Church of Saint-Etienne. (St. Stephan)

Metz, France, Cathedrale Saint-Etienne.

Moscow, Soviet Union, Tretiakov Gallery.

New York, New York, Metropolitan Opera, Lincoln Center.

New York, New York, Museum of Modern Art.

New York, New York, Solomon R. Guggenheim Museum.

New York, New York, United Nations.

Nice, France, Musée National Message Biblique Marc Chagall.

Nice, France, Université de Droit et Sciences Économiques.

Paris, France, Musée d'Art Moderne de la Ville de Paris.

Paris, France, Musée National d'Art Moderne,
    Centre Georges Pompidou.

Paris, France, Paris Opera House

Philadelphia, Pennsylvania, Philadelphia Museum of Art.

Pocantico Hills, New York, Pocantico Hills Chapel.

Prague, Czechoslovakia, Narodni Galerie v Prague.

Reims, France, Reims Cathedral.

Saint Louis, Missouri, Saint Louis Museum of Art.

Saint-Paul-de-Vence, France, Fondation Marguerite et Aimé Maeght.

Sarrebourg, France, Chapel of Penitents. (Cordeliers)

Tel Aviv, Israel, Tel Aviv Museum.

Tokyo, Japan, Galerie Tamenaga.

Toronto, Canada, Art Gallery of Ontario.

Zurich, Switzerland, Fraumünster Church.

Zurich, Switzerland, Kunsthaus Zurich.

Libraries for Research

Of course, there are public libraries in major cities with wonderful books on Chagall. University and college libraries and museums also offer reference materials for Chagall research.

Here, I list three that are not open to the public except by special request. You do not have to be doing research on Chagall in order for them to open their doors to you, but you must call beforehand and make arrangements to view their collection.

Art Institute of Chicago, Chicago, Illinois

The Ryerson Library of the Art Institute of Chicago has one of the most amazing Chagall book collections. Early documents from 1925 in the languages of Russian, French, Hebrew, and Italian abound in wonderful magazine articles, pamphlets, exhibition catalogues and books.

I spent two four-hour days going through the collection and found books that I had never seen before. Another added feature is the glorious dome of the Ryerson Library that was created by Tiffany.

Musée Marc Chagall, Nice, France

This library has numerous books and catalogues on Chagall and also has an extensive collection of books on religion and art. The staff is also very helpful.

J. Pierpont Morgan Library, New York, New York

This library has the letters, original documents, and business correspondence between Chagall and his new York art agent, Pierre Matisse. It is a beautiful collection written in French. It is a great opportunity to read original letters of Chagall written in his own handwriting regarding his paintings.

When Matisse died his wife Tana and her family arranged for this treasure to be in the hands of the J. Pierpont Morgan Library. Madame Matisse could not have made a better choice.

Examples of Small Libraries Open to the Public

Rhinelander, Wisconsin District Library has a wonderful collection of Chagall art books given to them by Dr. Warner S. Bump, one of the leading citizens of this small community. The Chagall collection is a memorial to his wife, and is an example that even in the northern part of Wisconsin you can find great Chagall art books.

The Sandhills Community College in Pinehurst, North Carolina, has a fantastic Chagall book collection. People who come to live in this area eventually donate their Chagall art books, along with other art books, to the college. North Carolina has a wonderful interstate and intrastate loan system.

If you are in a small community, do not forget to check out the local library for art books on Chagall. There are some great finds!

Magazine Articles

Artist at Work, Marc Chagall: by Carlton Lake

The Atlantic, July 1963

English

Pages 85-112

This article was a supplement in *The Atlantic* magazine by the American art critic Carlton Lake. The entire article is devoted to an interview with Chagall about his love of stained glass windows and his need to create stained glass windows in houses of worship. Along with the interview with Chagall, the author has included the thoughts of Charles Marq, the artisan for the Chagall windows.

I found this magazine through ABEBOOKS.com. They, in turn, located it at Vincent Parestianni Books, Penfield, New York. The cost of the magazine was ten dollars plus shipping. For a student of Chagall this was worth a hundred times more. A few copies of this magazine still may be available around the world.

Architectural Digest Visits Marc Chagall: by Charlotte Aillaud

Photography by Derry Moore

Architectural Digest, August 1984

English

Pages 75-81

A lovely and sweet article about Vava and Marc Chagall and their beautiful home in Saint-Paul-de-Vence. The photographs include pictures outside and inside of their house, as well as Chagall's atelier (studio). The most interesting aspect of this article is the artwork of other artists, Matisse, Renoir and Giacometti in their home.

The Chagall File: by Susan Josephs

ARTnews, May 1999

English

Pages 158-159

This article, which is a must read, is totally devoted to the research work of Yale Professor Benjamin Harshav, who discovered that the FBI documented Marc Chagall's political associations, activities, and perceived character traits – suspecting that he was overly friendly with the communists.

Chagall a communist? Harshav describes, "Chagall's relationship to communism as a flirtation." This article is so fascinating because it not only discusses Chagall, but also gives us a flavor of the times in America, the FBI, and the aftermath of the Cold War, and Chagall's comings and goings in the USA beginning in 1941.

Chagall's Christmas Gift: by Isabel Allende
translated by Tamara Glenny

Arts and Antiques, December 1989

English

Pages 84-86

This story, written by the world famous Latin American writer, has given us the gift of Chagall the person, through a simple reproduction of one of his paintings. This "painting," loaded with Chagallian themes, became the source of her "first love" – Chagall, that lasted a lifetime. Only a writer like Allende can put her love of Chagall in this most imaginative true story. You will love this story and remember it always.

The Elusive Marc Chagall: by Joseph A. Harriss

The Smithsonian, December 2003

English

Pages 88-96

Harriss has written a lovely biographical article on Chagall, with an interview with David McNeil, Chagall's son. His mother, Virginia Haggard Mc-Neil, was Chagall's companion from 1945-1952. The article has wonderful reproductions of some of Chagall's artwork, but most important includes some of the memories of David growing up with Chagall.

The author pays tribute to Chagall's 75-year career as an artist, during which time he produced an "astounding" 10,000 works! Well, I guess it is true, you can get older but you do not have to get old -- this is one of Chagall's great lessons.

Chagall: by Véronique Prat

Photos: Jean-Michel Voge

Le Figaro Magazine, July 7, 1984

French

Pages 52-57

This is a great article written in French. Unfortunately, the author has written that Chagall was 98 when she wrote the article in honor of his birthday. In fact he was 97 years old. However, the cover of the magazine honors Chagall with a great photo wearing the sweater that I bought him at Marshall Fields in Chicago the year before. Also another photo of this famous sweater is on page 57.

Only *Le Figaro Magazine*, could make Chagall open the door of his atelier and let the viewer in for some magnificent photos of the artist at work painting a circus theme. It is a beautiful interview by the author and one day should be translated into English.

Spreading Chagall's Message: by Laurie Altias

ARTnews, February 2000
English
Pages 152-156

This article is so fascinating because it proves the fact that when you are living and you give so much of yourself to the world that when you die, you go on living. The author of this article has presented a beautiful story of the Comité Chagall in Paris and its obligation to Marc Chagall and his artwork, from authenticating, reviewing reproductions, cataloguing and preparing exhibitions.

There is no end to Chagall. This article gives the reader a sense of the monumental work that Chagall did while he was alive and what it takes to keep it alive while he is no longer with us.

DVDs and Videos

The Emmy Award winning documentary filmmaker, the late Chuck Olin, produced *The Gift*. It is the 1974 documentary of *The Four Seasons* mosaic in Chicago. Detailed in every way with exquisite photography, the viewer learns how a mosaic is created by Chagall and the artisan Michel Tharin. We also see and hear Chagall giving his thoughts on life and love. This DVD is brilliant.

A Palette of Glass, the story of the *America Windows*, also produced by Chuck Olin and made in 1978, is a follow-up DVD to *The Gift*. This also taps into the world of making stained glass windows by the artisan Charles Marq. Marq and Chagall together are one giant genius. If anything, you will learn what makes a Chagall window a Chagall window.

1. The Gift (1974), Video and DVD

2. A Palette of Glass (1978), Video and DVD

3. Chagall (1964), Video

4. Homage to Chagall (1977), Video

5. Portrait of an Artist – Marc Chagall (1985), Video

6. Artists of the 20th Century: Marc Chagall (2004), Video

7. To Russia, Asses and Others (2004), DVD

Music CDs

A great deal of Chagall's life was elevated by music! I have listed three CDs. Perhaps there are more out there, but these are the three I know of. By listening to the music about Chagall one gets a deeper appreciation of his art.

Ode to Marc Chagall

Shimon Knoll and the Ensemble Europa©

1998 ZC Music Group, Inc.

Spandau, Germany

Shimon Knoll's Ode to Marc Chagall is a work of narrator, soprano, piano and small chamber orchestra and percussion. It is a musical gift to Chagall the poet, the lover and the great Jewish artist of the 20th century.

Homage to Chagall: The Chagall Windows

Mainz, Germany© 1990, VDE-Gallo

This homage to Chagall is for trumpets, mezzo-sopranos, quartets and organ. Four different composers inspired by the Biblical artwork of Chagall produced musical works that were written on different occasions. The composers, with diverse musical styles, have given the listener a new approach to the master of 20th century Biblical art.

Conversations with Chagall

The Chagall Suite

Conversations

Seth Weinstein composer and pianist

Produced by Vivian R. Jacobson, 2008

You will love this CD with its eight-part composition, brilliantly composed by Seth Weinstein of New York. Ralph and I commissioned this music for our 50th wedding anniversary. Seth has captured the major themes of Chagall artwork. This CD can be purchased through cdbaby.com/cd/ sethweinstein or by phone 1-800-289-6923, and the music can also be downloaded. For a listing of live concerts given by Seth Weinstein in the United States and abroad at which he performs the music on this CD, go to the website: www.vivianjacobson.com.

Those who have bought this CD hear the messages of Chagall's hope, peace, reconciliation and love through this original music. The themes are:

Vitebsk

The Bible

The Circus

Lovers and Flowers

The Prince of Peace – Jesus and the Prophet of Peace – Isaiah

Paris

Nature

Angels

The other part of the CD is a musical conversation between Elvis Presley and Chagall based on my lecture on Elvis and Chagall. This composition premiered in Memphis, Tennessee on August 21, 2005, honoring the anniversary of Elvis' passing. It is a fusion of jazz, rock and roll, blues, klezmer and grand Russian themes.

You can almost hear and see Chagall drinking a glass of tea and Elvis drinking a Coke side by side at a café table and having a wonderful conversation about their lives.

Postcard Books

I encourage parents and grandparents to buy Chagall postcard books for children and teenagers. They are inexpensive, and the children love the Chagallian colors, the animals and floating figures. While we show art books to young children, it basically is a "keep your hands off" policy. But with postcards the children can touch and feel a postcard while discussing what he says and feels with parents or friends. Here are my favorites.

Jerusalem Window Postcard Book – 24 postcards

Dover Publications, Inc., Minneola, New York

1993

English

ISBN0-486-27479

This postcard book devoted to *The Twelve Tribes of Israel* is outstanding. This publication has the final gouache for the stained glass window and the stained glass window side by side. The reader can view the interpretation of a window from a gouache that gives excellent color and reproductions.

As of this year the book is no longer available, but hunt it down through yard sales or used bookstores. The book includes full Biblical stories from *Genesis* and *Deuteronomy* in regard to the twelve tribes and a great short biography of Chagall.

Chagall: A Postcard Book – 30 postcards

The Running Press, Philadelphia, Pennsylvania

1990

English

ISBN 0-89471-806-1

The outstanding feature of this postcard book is the introductory biography of Chagall. It is so special and so well written that I asked The Running Press to grant permission for me to reprint it as a handout for my lectures. Heavy quality paper is used for the postcards. This one is great for children ages 3-6.

Marc Chagall – 18 postcards

Prestel-Verlag, Münich-New York

1995

German and English

ISBN 3-7913-1457-2

This book is a wonderful selection of Chagall artwork, including cards of lithographs from Daphne and Chloe and a good biography.

Marc Chagall – 30 postcards

Taschen Verlag Publishing House

1998

German, French and Italian

ISBN 3-82128-7968-1

Taschen is known for wonderful reproductions. A great selection of Chagall's most famous paintings.

Marc Chagall: St. Stephan Windows – 18 postcards

Kunstverlag Postcard Book No. 85

2001

Bonn, Germany

Maria Laach

German

ISBN 3-930990-81-4

Klaus Mayer, the priest that commissioned the St. Stephan Windows for the church in Mainz, has written a lovely one page spiritual introduction to Marc Chagall. The postcards achieve the exact coloring of the Biblical windows. The blue colors of Chagall were a symbol of hope. You may want to keep this little book bedside. It is very inspirational and when holding it you feel that you have a prayer book in hand, as opposed to a postcard book.

Internet Sites – Where to Buy Books Old and New, Catalogues, DVDs, CDs, Videos, Posters and Visuals

- **amazon.com** – books and catalogues
- **abebooks.com**- books and catalogues (They will find a book dealer that will be able to help you locate specific reading material).
- **alibris.com** – books and catalogues
- **allposters.com** – posters, framed, unframed and wonderful reproductions

- **artcyclopedia.com** – listings of Chagall art works worldwide
- **davisartslides.com** - slides
- **olinfilms.com** - Chagall documentary films

Posters and Photos

In my laundry room I have a picture of Chagall photographed when he was at our house in 1974. The photo hangs above the ironing board. One time when I visited Chagall we began to talk about music and how we both loved Mozart. Chagall then said, "Schubert makes me want to paint," and I replied, "and Chagall makes me want to iron." Did he laugh!

Good quality photos and posters can bring as much happiness as an original artwork. Posters make wonderful gifts for the bride and groom and as a house warming present. Fantastic reproductions can be bought on the Internet at **allposters.com**. Photos can be found on Internet sites and bookstores.

THE DISCOVERED AND UNDISCOVERED CHAGALL

(Dates are Circa)

Chagall is loved the world over, from Japan to Europe, and from Israel to the United States. Here are his works open to the public:

1. USA: JOB, tapestry, Rehabilitation Institute of Chicago, Chicago, Illinois, 1982-1985.
2. USA: THE FOUR SEASONS, mosaic, First National Bank Plaza, Chicago, Illinois, 1973-1974.
3. USA: THE AMERICA WINDOWS, stained glass, Art Institute of Chicago, Chicago, Illinois, 1978.
4. USA: THE PROPHET JEREMIAH, tapestry, Helfaer Jewish Community Center, Milwaukee, Wisconsin. 1958-1959.
5. USA: THE UNION CHURCH, stained glass, Rockefeller Chapel, Pocantico Hills, New York, 1963-1966.
6. USA: THE PEACE WINDOW, stained glass, United Nations, New York, 1963
7. USA: THE SOURCE OF MUSIC, THE TRIUMPH OF MUSIC, murals, Metropolitan Opera House, Lincoln Center, New York, 1966.

8. ENGLAND: CHICHESTER CHURCH WINDOWS, stained glass, Chichester, England, 1978.

9. ENGLAND: THE ALL SAINTS CHURCH WINDOWS, stained glass, Tudley, England, 1967, 1974-1978.

10. FRANCE: THE STORY OF BABY MOSES, mosaic, baptistery of the Cathedral, Vence, France, 1979.

11. FRANCE: THE CHAGALL HARPSICHORD, replica of an 18th century French Blanchet harpsichord, with inside of instrument painted with the love story of Rebecca and Isaac, by Marc Chagall, Musée Chagall, Nice, France,1981.

12. FRANCE: THE PROPHET ELIJAH, mosaic, Musée Chagall, Nice, France, 1973.

13. FRANCE: THE CREATION OF THE WORLD, stained glass, Musée Chagall, Nice, France, 1973.

14. FRANCE: THE ENTRANCE TAPESTRY, Musée Chagall, Nice, France, 1973.

15. FRANCE: LE REPAS DES ANGES, mosaic, La Chapelle-Roseline, Les Arcs sur Argens, France, 1975.

16. FRANCE: THE PEACE WINDOW, stained glass, Chapelle des Cordeliers, Sarrebourg, France, 1976.

17. FRANCE: THE PEACE TAPESTRY, woven after the Peace Windows at the United Nations, Chapelle des Cordeliers, Sarrebourg, France, 1994.

18. FRANCE: THE MOSAIC, exterior wall of the Library Foundation Maeght, St. Paul de Vence, France, 1964-1965.

19. FRANCE: PARIS OPERA HOUSE, ceiling mural, Paris, France, 1964

20. FRANCE: THE MESSAGE OF ODYSSEUS, wall mosaic, Faculty of the Law School, University of Nice, France, 1967-1968.

21. FRANCE: THE CROSSING OF THE RED SEA, stained glass, Church of the Notre Dame-de-Toute de Grace du Plateau D'Assy, France, 1956.

22. FRANCE: HEADSTONE IN BRONZE OF YVAN GOLL. Père Lachaise Cemetery, Division 10 – Section 10, Paris, France, 1950.

23. FRANCE: THE SIX WINDOWS ON NATURE, stained glass, The Village Church, Le Saillant de Voutezac, Limousin, France. 1978-1982.

24. GERMANY: COMÉDIE OF THE ARTS, reception hall mural, Frankfurt Theater, Frankfurt, Germany, 1959.
25. GERMANY: ST. STEPHAN WINDOWS, stained glass, Mainz, Germany, 1977-1984.
26. ISRAEL: MOSAIC AT THE KNESSET, Jerusalem, Israel, 1964-1965.
27. ISRAEL: TAPESTRY AT THE KNESSET, reception hall entry, Jerusalem, Israel, 1963-1964, Exodus, 1963, Isaiah's Prophecy, 1968.
28. ISRAEL; THE TWELVE TRIBES OF ISRAEL, stained glass, The Hadassah Hospital Synagogue, Jerusalem, Israel, 1961.
29. SWITZERLAND: THE FRAUMÜNSTER WINDOWS, stained glass, Zurich, Switzerland, 1971.

The Fifteen Stained Glass Windows of Marc Chagall
as listed by the Union Church of Pocantico Hills, Pocantico Hills, New York
1957-1978

UNITED STATES

Union Church of Pocantico Hills, New York 1953-66

United Nations Secretariat, New York, New York, 1963

The Art Institute of Chicago, Chicago, Illinois, 1976-79

ISRAEL

Hadassah Hebrew University Medical Center, Jerusalem, Israel, 1960-62

GERMANY

St. Stephan Parish Church, Mainz, Germany, 1977-84

SWITZERLAND

Fraumünster Church, Zurich, Switzerland, 1969-70

ENGLAND

All Saints Church, Tudeley, Kent, England, 1967, 1974-78

144

Chichester Cathedral, Sussex, England, 1978

FRANCE

Notre-Dame de Toute Grace (Baptistery), Plateau D'Assy. Savoy, France, 1957

Metz Cathedral, Metz, France, 1959

Abbatiale – Saint Pierre, Moissac, France, 1962

Musée National Message Biblique Marc Chagall, Nice, France, 1971-72

Reims Cathedral, Reims, France, 1973-74

Chapelle des Cordeliers, Sarrebourg, Moselle, France, 1976-78

Village Church, Le Saillant, France, 1978-82

IN CHRONOLOGICAL ORDER

Notre-Dame de Toute Grace, France 1957

Metz Cathedral, France 1959

Abbatiale Saint-Pierre, France 1962

Hadassah Hebrew University Medical Center, Israel 1960-62

Union Church of Pocantico Hills, United States 1963-66

United Nations Secretariat, United States 1963

Fraumünster Church, Switzerland 1969-70

Musée National Message Biblique Marc Chagall, France 1971-72

Reims Cathedral, France 1973-74

All Saints Church, England 1974-78

The Art Institute of Chicago, United States 1976-79

Chapelle des Cordeliers, France 1976-78

St. Stephan Church, Germany 1977-84

Village Church, France 1978-82

Chichester Cathedral, England 1978

Speeches
Speech given on welcoming Marc Chagall
as a Hadassah Associate at our home in Chicago
September 29, 1974
(Speech delivered in French and English)

On behalf of my family and Mr. and Mrs. Dellsey, our president of Hadassah, Mr. and Mrs. Rosenstein and Mrs. Goldberg, we welcome you to our home.

The Hadassah Hospital in Israel is a project that speaks of peace for medical services for Israel and all the world. The Chagall windows in our synagogue inspire the women and the men's association of Hadassah to dedicate their lives for the betterment of humanity and Israel.

We are very happy to present to you this commemorative plaque of membership in Hadassah on this day, the 29th of September 1974. And now Maître Chagall, friend of the world, you are a Hadassah Associate. Congratulations.

Dedication of the Chagall Harpsichord
(In the inside cover, Chagall painted the love story
of Rebecca and Isaac)
January 4, 1981
(Speech delivered in French)

Esteemed dear Maître Chagall and dear Madame Chagall, Mr. President, Ambassador of the United States, Minister of Culture, Director of the Museum, Ladies and Gentlemen:

I am here today on behalf of the American Friends of Chagall's Biblical Message Museum. It is a great honor and privilege to join with you for the presentation and dedication of this beautiful harpsichord that has been painted so magnificently by Marc Chagall. The Biblical Message is a unique museum and was created by the world's greatest living artist as a testimony to the enduring human spirit.

It is our friend Marc Chagall who has said of this museum and of his paintings "that I want to leave these paintings in this house so that people may find here a certain peace, a certain spirituality, a religious atmosphere, a feeling for life, . . . and perhaps the young and the less young will come

146

to this house seeking for an ideal of love and brotherhood such as my colour and line have dreamed of."

These words of Marc Chagall are reflected upon at a time when man is searching for peace of mind, self-reflection, fulfillment of spirit and hope. These ideals form a common bond for truth in the world of art, literature, poetry and music.

Man is constantly attempting to express himself in the arts. For most of us, creativity remains locked within ourselves. The inability to express creativity can be alleviated by listening to a great symphony or a tranquil sonata, by viewing a glorious painting, or perhaps, by reading a touching poem.

The spirit of the arts promotes and magnifies the need for man to live in a peaceful world so that his hopes may continue to be fulfilled every day of his life. The arts provide the necessary directions for one person to transmit his feelings to another person.

The artist, musician and poet express the ultimate ideals of a dream. People who live with the reality of problems and complexities of the world try to incorporate the ideals of the artist in their daily lives. The arts bring together people with different traditions, cultures, heritages and religious beliefs in an environment of understanding and the hope for peace.

It is with great enthusiasm for the arts that the members of the American Friends of Chagall's Biblical Message Museum have donated this harpsichord.

It is written in the book of Genesis, chapter 24, verse 67, in Hebrew – "And Isaac brought her into his mother Sarah's tent, and took Rebecca, and she became his wife; and he loved her." (Recited in Hebrew and French.)

May the message of eternal love of Rebecca and Isaac so wondrously painted by Marc Chagall and the sounds of music that will come forth from this harpsichord continue to inspire beauty and understanding and peace throughout the world.

Speech presented at the Rehabilitation Institute of Chicago Dinner in honor of the dedication of the *Job* tapestry June 19, 1986

Honored guests, The Friends of the Chagall Tapestry want to thank you for your cooperation and confidence in our committee to bring this tapestry to Chicago and to the Rehabilitation Institute.

This morning at the presentation on behalf of the Friends of the Chagall Tapestry, today we presented to you this gift, a work of art designed by our beloved friend Marc Chagall and woven by Yvette Cauquil-Prince. These two great artists and our committee have devoted ourselves to the disabled and the handicapped for the last four years.

This project has not been an easy one and as chairman I can honestly tell you that things were extremely difficult and in a way I was disabled many times by incredible and unbelievable complications.

If this tapestry is our gift to you, then it is your spirit of courage, perseverance and commitment to a better and more productive life that has been your gift to us. You have inspired us for having been involved in bringing the tapestry here to the Rehabilitation Institute and enriched our lives and the lives of all those who have participated as contributors.

And to the employees of the hospital, the mail room, secretary, accounting, public relations and those directly and indirectly involved with this tapestry project, we thank you. For without your extraordinary help this project never would have become a reality. You have made our dream come true.

Speech presented to the Rehabilitation Institute of Chicago and their families and friends at the dedication of the *Job* tapestry June 20, 1986

Dear friends, what a special day this is in our lives. One filled with joy, hope and inspiration for a better and more peaceful world. We will remember this day always in our hearts and in our minds, for it has brought all of us together to witness the dream of our committee and that will be shared for years to come by thousands. For the Friends of the Chagall Tapestry whom, with their intelligent, creative minds, commitment and perseverance, a dream has come true.

The third major artwork of Marc Chagall for our city, was designed by the artist and woven by Yvette Cauquil-Prince. Only the idealists made reality possible for the realists.

For the Rehabilitation Institute of Chicago, thank you for the home for our dream. For Vava Chagall, our thanks in helping in every way and for guiding us with your ideas and suggestions. For Yvette Cauquil-Prince, our thanks for your beautiful interpretation of Chagall and for being with us every step of the way from the very first day four years ago. And to our friend Marc Chagall, who gave us the spiritual message.

"Mais dans l'art comme dans la vie tout est possible si a la base il y a l'amour."

"But in art, as in life, everything is possible, so long as it is based on love."

May his memory be a blessing forever. Blessed art Thou, O Lord our God, King of the Universe, who has given us life, sustained us, and enabled us to reach this moment in time. Amen.

Speech presented for the 25th Anniversary
of the passing of Marc Chagall
Union Church Pocantico Hills, Tarrytown, New York
March 28, 2010
and the Musée Chagall, Nice, France September 25, 2010

Today we memorialize the 25th anniversary of the passing of Marc Chagall, a true citizen of the world. The gift that Marc Chagall gave to the world in his art and in his writings was the message of hope, peace, reconciliation and love, and all of this through paintings, murals, tapestries, illustrated books, ceramics, stained glass windows and theater sets and more artistic forms.

The survivor of pogroms, anti-Semitism, the Russian Revolution, two world wars, and an escapee from the Nazis in 1941, Chagall still had hope for humanity and reconciliation.

He never exhibited hate or anger for his oppressors. The way the world affected him personally deepened his determination to pour out his love for all people and to strive for understanding, hope and peace.

He brought this love to us in every artwork. Some people give so much to the world while they are living that when they are no longer on this earth they continue to live in the hearts and minds of mankind.

Such was the distinction and legacy of Marc Chagall.

May his memory be a blessing forever.

The Friends of the Chagall Tapestry Committee
Rehabilitation Institute of Chicago
1982 – 1986

John H. Bryan, Jr., Honorary Chairman

Vivian R. Jacobson, Chairman

Members

Pamela Bernstein
Simon Bernstein
Jonna Wood - Prince Chewning
Harriette Coleman
Leonard Coleman
Janice R. Davis
Susan P. Doane
Bradley B. Falkof
Sheila Goldberg
Anne Goodwin
Blair Hull
Ralph Jacobson
Robert L. Lauer
Jo Ann Lazuka
Hector Richard Loya
Regina E. Manley
Cynthia McLachlan
Marvin Moss
Jonathan Plotkin
Robin Plotkin
Elizabeth Ragan
Elliot D. Rawls
John B. Reilly
Pat Rich
Alice P. Robinson
Mary Roland
Ben Rosenthal
Lorelei Rosenthal
Jeffrey M. Schecter
Elly Wilder

BIBLIOGRAPHY

BOOKS

Alexander, Sidney. *Chagall.* New York, New York: G.P. Putnam's Sons, 1978.

Amiel, Leon, Publisher. *Chagall in Jerusalem.* New York, New York: Leon Amiel Publisher, 1983.

Antonova, Irina, Andréi Voznesensky and Marina Bessonova. *Chagall Discovered.* New York, New York: Hugh Lauter Levin Associates, Inc., 1988.

Baal-Teshuva, Jacob. *Marc Chagall.* Cologne, Germany: Benedict Taschen Verlag GmbH, 1998.

—. *Marc Chagall: Tapestries.* Köln, London, Madrid, New York, Paris, Tokyo: Benedict Taschen Verlag GmbH, 1999.

—. *Chagall: A Retrospective.* Hugh Lauter Levin Associates, Inc., New York, 1995.

Bober, Natalie S. *Marc Chagall: Painter of Dreams.* Philadelphia, Pennsylvania: The Jewish Publication Society, 1991.

Bohm-Duchen, Monica. *Chagall.* London, England: Phaidon Press Limited, 1998.

Chagall, Bella. *Burning Lights.* New York, New York: Biblio Press, 1996.

Chagall, Marc. *Marc Chagall: My Life.* New York, New York: The Orion Press, 1960.

Cramer, Gérald (Editor). *Marc Chagall: Poèmes*. Geneva, Switzerland: Cramer Éditeur, 1975.

de La Fontaine, Jean. *Marc Chagall: Fables of La Fontaine*. New York, New York: The New Press, 1995.

Doschka, Roland (Editor). *Marc Chagall: Origins and Paths*. Munich - New York: Prestel-Verlag, 1998.

Durham, John I. *The Biblical Rembrandt: Human Painter in a Landscape of Faith*. Macon, Georgia: Mercer University Press, 2004.

Erben, Walter. *Marc Chagall*. New York - Washington: Frederick A. Praeger, Publishers, 1957.

Forestier, Sylvie. *Chagall - Keramik*. München, Germany: Hirmer Verlag, 1990.

Freund, Miriam. *Jewels for a Crown: The Story of the Chagall Windows*. New York, Toronto, London: McGraw-Hill Book Company, Inc., 1963.

Gauss, Ulrike (Editor). *Marc Chagall: The Lithographs*. New York, New York: D.A.P., 1998.

Genauer, Emily. *Chagall at the "Met"*. New York, New York: Chagall and Metropolitan Opera Association, Inc., Tudor Publishing Company, 1971.

Goldmann, Christoph. *Das Gelb auf Davids Harfe*. Stuttgart, Germany: Verlag Katholisches Bibelwerk, 2004.

—. *Bild-Zeichen bei Marc Chagall Alphabetische Enzyklopadie der Bildzeichen*. Göttingen, Germany: Vandenhoeck & Ruprecht, 1995.

—. *Message Biblique Marc Chagall - Der Bildemidrasch Eines Judischen Malers Zur Hebraischen Bibel - Textband, Band I: Analyse und Interpreation.* Heidelberg, Germany: Ruprecht-Karls-Universitat zu Heidelberg, 1989.

—. *Message Biblique Marc Chagall - Der Bildemidrasch Eines Judischen Malers Zur Hebraischen Bibel - Bildband, Band II: Bild und Textdokumentation.* Heidelberg, Germany: Ruprecht-Karls-Universitat zu Heidelberg, 1989.

Grasnick, Ulrich. *Hungrig von Traümen Gedichte.* Berlin, Germany: Verlag der Nation, Berlin, 1990.

Greenfield, Howard. *Marc Chagall.* New York, New York: Harry N. Abrams, Energy Publications, 1990.

Haftman, Werner. *Chagall.* New York, New York: Henry N. Abrams, Inc., 1984.

Haggard, Virginia. *My Life with Chagall: Seven Years of Plenty with the Master as Told by the Woman Who Shared Them.* New York, New York: Donald Fine, Inc., 1986.

Harshav, Benjamin (Editor). *Marc Chagall on Art and Culture.* Stanford, California: Stanford University Press, 2003.

—. *Marc Chagall and His Times: A Documentary.* Stanford, California: Stanford University Press, 2004.

—. *Marc Chagall on the Lost Jewish World.* New York, New York: Rizzoli, 1996.

Ikonen-Museum. *Als Chagall das Fliegen lernte.* Frankfurt am Main, Germany: Legat - Verlag Frankfurt, 2004.

Kagan, Andrew. *Chagall.* New York, New York: Abbeville Press, 1989.

Keller, Horst. *Marc Chagall, Life and Works.* Woodbury, New York: Barron's Educational Series, Inc., 1980.

Lamarche, Helene. *Chagall for Children.* Montreal, Canada: The Montreal Museum of Fine Arts, 1989.

Landmann, Bimba. *I Am Marc Chagall.* Grand Rapids, Michigan: Eerdmans Books for Young Readers, 2006.

Malraux, André. *Anti-Memoirs.* New York, Chicago, San Francisco: Holt, Rinehart and Winston, Inc., 1968.

Marteau, Robert. *Stained Glass Windows of Chagall 1957 - 1970.* New York, New York: Tudor Publishing Company, 1973.

Mayer, Klaus. *Heaven and the Highest Heavens Cannot Contain You.* Wurzburg, Germany: Echter Publishing House, 1996.

—. *I Have Set My Bow in the Clouds.* Wurzburg, Germany: Echter Publishing House, 1995.

—. *Lord, My God, How Great You Are!* Wurzburg, Germany: Echter Publishing House, 1995.

—. *The God of the Fathers.* Wurzburg, Germany: Echter Publishing House, 1993.

Meisler, Stanley. *Shocking Paris - Soutine, Chagall and The Outsiders of Montparnasse.* New York, New York: Palgrave MacMillan® Trade, 2015.

Meyer, Franz. *Marc Chagall.* New York, New York: Harry N. Abrams, Inc., 1963 - 1964.

Moldovan, Kurt, *Einfürimg von Arabische Nachte*. München, Germany: R. Piper & Co. Verlag, 1958.

Provoyeur, Pierre. *Marc Chagall: Biblical Interpretations*. New York and London: Alpine Fine Arts Collections, LTD, 1983.

Riedy, James L. *Chicago Sculpture*. Chicago, Illinois: University of Illinois Press, 1981.

Schapiro, Meyer. *Modern Art: 19th and 20th Centuries*, Selected Papers. New York, New York: George Braziller, Inc. , 1979.

Sorlier, Charles (Editor). *Chagall by Chagall*. New York, New York: Harry N. Abrams, Inc., 1979.

Turner, Paul. *Marc Chagall: Daphnis and Chloe*. Münich - New York: Prestel-Verlag, 1994.

Venezia, Mike. *Marc Chagall*. New York, New York: Children's Press: A division of Grolier Publishing, 2000.

Walther, Ingo F. and Metzger, Rainer. *Marc Chagall: Painting as Poetry*. Cologne, Germany: Taschen, 2006.

Wilson, Jonathan. *Marc Chagall*. New York, New York: Shocken Press and Nextbook, 2007.

CATALOGUES: Museum and Art Galleries

Chagall. Zurich, Switzerland: Kunsthaus Zurich, (May 6 - July 30, 1967).

Chagall. Philadelphia, Pennsylvania: Philadelphia Museum of Art, (1985).

Chagall. Köln, Germany: Galerie: Orangerie-Reinz, (1982).

Chagall from Russia to Paris. Boca Raton, Florida: Boca Raton Museum of Art, (January - February 2002).

Chagall und Deutschland. Frankfurt, Germany: The Jewish Museum of Frankfurt, (February 1 - 18 and May 1 - August 1, 2004).

Chagall: Die Mythen der Bible. Vienna, Austria: Albertina Museum, (December 2, 2004 - March 28, 2005).

Chagall: Love and the Stage. London, England: Royal Academy of Arts, (July 2 - October 4, 1998).

Chagall-Vitebsk, St. Petersburg, Paris. Paris, France: Galerie Gérald Piltzer, (March 5 - May 8, 1993).

Marc Chagall. Montreal, Canada: The Montreal Museum of Fine Arts, (October 28, 1988 - February 26, 1989).

Marc Chagall. San Francisco, California: San Francisco Museum of Modern Art, (2003).

Marc Chagall. Beverly Hills, California: Timothy Yarger Fine Arts, (1999).

Marc Chagall. Vitebsk, Belarus: Museum of Arts of Vitebsk, Belarus, (1997).

Marc Chagall and the Jewish Theater. New York, New York: Guggenheim Museum, (September 23, 1992 - January 17, 1993).

Marc Chagall zum 100. Geburtstag Gouachen und Aquarelle. Balingen, Germany: Hermann Daniel GmbH & Co. KG, Balingen, (1986).

Marc Chagall: 1907 - 1917. Berne, Switzerland and New York, New York: Museum of Fine Arts Berne, Jewish Museum in New York City., (December 2, 1995 - February 28, 1996).

Marc Chagall: Les Années Russes, 1907 - 1922. Paris, France: Musée d'Art Moderne, (April 13 - September 17, 1995).

Marc Chagall: Oeuvres sur Papier. Paris, France: Musée National d'art Moderne-Centre Georges Pompidou, (June 30 - October 8, 1984).

Marc Chagall: Retrospective de l'oeuvre peint. Saint-Paul de Vence France: Fondation Maeght Saint-Paul, (1984).

Marc Chagall: The Four Seasons. New York, New York: Pierre Matisse Gallery, (May 1975).

Marc Chagall: Vitraux et Sculptures. Paris, France: Editions de la Reunion des Musées nationaux, (1984).

National Museum Message Biblique Marc Chagall. Paris, France: Editions de la Reunion des Musées nationaux, (1976).

The Dixon Gallery and Gardens. Memphis, Tennessee: The Dixon Gallery and Gardens, (1996).

ARTICLES: Magazines and Newspapers

Aillaud, Charlotte. *Architectural Digests Visits: Marc Chagall.* Architectural Digest August 1984: 75-81.

Allende, Isabel. *Chagall's Christmas Gift.* Arts and Antiques December 1989: 84-86.

Altias, Laurie. *Spreading Chagall's Message.* ARTnews February 2000: 152-156.

Harriss, Joseph A. *The Elusive Marc Chagall.* The Smithsonian December 2003: 88-96.

Josephs, Susan. *The Chagall File.* ARTnews 1984 August: 158-159.

Lake, Carlton. *Artist at Work: Chagall.* The Atlantic July 1963: 85-112.

Prat, Veronique. *Chagall.* Le Figaro *Magazine* 7 July 1984: 52-57.

Wechsler, Rachael. *Chagall and the Village: The Affect of the Unrealistic.* Discoveries: Cornell University Spring 2007: 75-80.

CD/MUSIC

Jacobson, Vivian R. and Seth Weinstein. *Conversations with Chagall.* 2008.

DVD/FILM

The Monumental Art of Marc Chagall: The Four Seasons Mosaic, and the America Windows. Chuck Olin Associates, Inc. 2003.

Chagall's Journey. Directed by Randolph Wands. With Chaim Potok 1985. Documentary profiling the life of modern artist Marc Chagall.

About The Author

VIVIAN R. JACOBSON

Vivian Jacobson was a lifelong resident of Chicago until 1989 when she and her husband, a retired tax attorney, moved to Pinehurst, North Carolina. She received a BS degree in Elementary Education from Roosevelt University in Chicago, supplemented by post graduate studies in physical education, and in French language, culture and literature. A lifetime interest in art was nurtured by trips to the Art Institute of Chicago, where she first became acquainted with the works of Marc Chagall.

Photo courtesy of Glenn Sides

In 1974, the Jacobsons hosted a reception for Madame and Maître Chagall on behalf of the Hadassah Medical Organization of Jerusalem, and shortly thereafter, Vivian Jacobson became a founding member of the American Friends of Chagall's Biblical Message Museum in Nice, France. She initially served as secretary and became the president in 1978, a post she held until 1982.

Chagall and the French association were seeking additional financial support for the museum's exhibitions, concerts and library expansion, an undertaking which Vivian Jacobson was able to accomplish successfully. She also led a campaign for the purchase of a replica of an 18th century Blanchet harpsichord. Chagall painted the biblical story of Rebecca and Isaac on the inside cover of the instrument, and it was dedicated in 1981 as a testament to Chagall's belief that the integration of art and music would create world peace.

Vivian Jacobson was honored to work closely with Chagall on major international projects during the last eleven years of his life. Among them was heading up the fundraising committee to present a Chagall tapestry to the Rehabilitation Institute of Chicago in 1986. Woven by Yvette Cauquil-Prince of Paris, the masterful *Job* tapestry was commissioned by the Friends of the Chagall Tapestry.

In 2001, Vivian Jacobson was appointed a speaker on Marc Chagall for the North Carolina Humanities Council Forum and the grant was extended through 2018. She has lectured for art groups, museums, churches, synagogues, colleges and schools nationally as well as in Europe and Israel.

www.vivianjacobson.com